The Other Book Addiction;
A Thinking Disease

The Other Book Addiction; A Thinking Disease

Dr. Kenneth G Wilson

http://www.dockennethwilson.com
Designed by Chelsea Jones (me@chelseajonesdesigns.com)
Published by

Library of Congress Cataloging-in-Publication Data
ISBN 13: 9781548221676
Illustrations by Adrian Sky Rogers
ISBN: 1548221678

Acknowledgements

To my wife, Joyce Tigart Wilson: thank you for tolerating my slavish devotion to completing this book, which has its roots in the 1990s.

To my family, friends, colleagues, and patients: thank you for prodding me to complete this project.

To my exceptional daughters, Kellie and Lisa: thank you for your support. Also, I must acknowledge the role Lisa's passing inadvertently played in setting all of this in motion.

Thanks to all of the scientists who preceded and inspired me. *Good science brings paradigm shifts*. Galileo, Copernicus, Pasteur, Freud, Skinner, Beck, J. Young, and Watson and Crick changed the zeitgeist of whole fields by creating paradigm shifts. Felliti and Anda, among others, will get well-deserved credit for providing the impetus to change how we view addiction, its etiology, and its treatment.

To those dedicated to the pursuit of knowledge and the relief of human suffering caused by the unavoidable and unintended consequences of the vicissitudes of the environments we are subjected to as neonates, I offer you my thanks.

To those who highlight the need to provide adequate information to prospective parents about how susceptible children are to harm.

To those who honestly shared their histories with me. In doing so, you helped me to understand mine. To each of the people who risked disclosure of their traumas, which have been kept hidden from view. Thank you for having the courage to confront those traumas, understand their impact on you, and develop the skills to eliminate their control of your self-destructive behavior.

To all of my teachers who expected me to prove the validity of my suppositions and gave me much-needed praise, raised my self-esteem, and validated my obsession with "asking good questions."

To all of the tortured souls who ever hurt themselves because they didn't think they deserved better.

To the residents and staff of the Asklepion Therapeutic Community of the US penitentiary in Marion, Illinois, whose therapeutic skills taught me what psychotherapy can do.

To all of the therapeutic communities (TCs) who built my repertoire of treatment skills: Asklepion, Cenikor, the Stout Street Foundation Inc., and CRP) at the Salvation Army's City of Hope in Sarasota, Florida.

This book would not have been written without my being immersed in AA dogma, with its defiant reliance on the disease model of addiction.

My Grandson, Adrian Sky Rogers for his illustrations, My Granddaughter by marriage, Chelsea Jones for her help with packaging the manuscript and building my website and Keri who had the misfortune of being my editor. Thanks to all of you.

Preface

have been retired since 2004. My active affiliation to the addiction field has consisted of providing continuing clinical supervision and support to the Stout Street Foundation, Inc., and my inadvertent decision to volunteer clinical services to the Community Recovery Program (CRP) of the Salvation Army's City of Hope in Sarasota, Florida.

I have not submitted this book to any of the many professionals who I think would write a foreword for me because we are all on the same or related pages regarding where addiction treatment *should* be. Unfortunately, the cat has been successfully kept in the bag since before the '70s. I refer to the work of esteemed colleagues, including Dr. Eric Berne's *Games People Play*; Lee Robins's data on the voluntary cessation of heroin addiction among returning Vietnam veterans; Dr. Bruce Alexander's pioneering work in the Rat Park study; Dr. Claude Steiner's *Games Alcoholics Play*; Dr. Jeffery Young's development of Early Maladaptive Schemas (EMS's); and the perspicacity displayed by Dr. Felitti while analyzing data obtained from observations of obese patients that enabled our understanding of the well-documented relationship between adverse childhood experiences (ACEs) and self-destructive behavior, such as substance use disorders (SUDs).

From the constant references to family-of-origin issues in the *Diagnostic and Statistical Manual of Mental Disorders*, Fifth Edition (DSM-5), we know that the many faces of trauma are the precursors of most mental disorders and self-destructive behavior. We know that mental disorders precede most SUDs and co-occur with other mental health disorders, but we don't treat them concurrently. Why not? I see the results of trauma in the patients I treat all the time—their pain, the destruction in their lives, and the disruption in the lives of those around them—and attribute the *thinking disorder* to a *brain disease*. Most clinicians don't seem to acknowledge that patients hurt themselves the most. Why is this?

One of the reasons is that the Brain Disease Model of Addiction (BDMA) has had such a grip on medical, psychological, and substance-abuse counselors' education and overall training that little credence or attention has been given to psychological precursors. Another is that the disease model has focused on the search for a pharmacological solution (medicine) for a *thinking disorder*. Therefore, the treatment hasn't moved far from attempts at using pharmacological cocktails and lending grudging support to cognitive behavior therapy (CBT). Indeed, most treatment is meted out by recovering addicts subscribing to twelve-step programs. Alcoholics Anonymous (AA) advocates that because one is powerless to control one's behavior, one must depend on a higher power to obtain sobriety. Of course, this belief system completely ignores a human being's ability to make a choice. Why?

The "hijacked brain," and the "compulsive drug seeking"" caused by structural and functional changes to the brain, supposedly renders one incapable of choice. This is called reductionism. Explaining the workings of the *mind* by examining the *brain* takes us back to the nature versus nurture controversy; however, this is not viewed on a level playing field. The age-old expression *follow the money* explains the direction of the research. Congress controls the dispersion of funds to the scientific community, and because Congress wants to see something they can hold in their hands, the money goes to hard science, which supplies brain scans they can see and touch. To view the position more completely, see Sally Satel and Scott O. Lillienfeld's article "Addiction and the Brain-Disease Fallacy," which states that "the brain-disease model obscures the dimension of choice in addiction...Thankfully, addicts can choose to recover and are not helpless victims of their own 'hijacked brains.'"[1]

Caveat 1: the style I have used to present my argument is unorthodox. The use of boldface, italics, and different fonts and font sizes is for emphasis.

Caveat 2: in service of transparency, many sources of objective scientific facts have been made available with Internet citation so that you may consult them directly. This is a stylistic faux pas. However, I prefer you to have easy access to these original sources. PubMed and NCBI are scientific journal sites where anyone can gain access to journal articles.

I have provided constant references to Wikipedia regarding synopses of sources, which you may wish to review for a more complete understanding of the perspectives presented. I prefer original sources, so they are available for your perusal. Ask the experts!

This book is another attempt to change the existing paradigm of the so-called *broken brain* by reintroducing the *disordered mind* into the discussion of self-destructive behavior. In light of major findings, it is arrogant to continue to ignore the mind's ability to make decisions that affect the brain simply because there aren't any pictures of the mind (although there is lots of data). It is irresponsible, especially in light of the human suffering caused by early abuse and neglect, to continue to cling to outdated belief systems. Moreover, this book's purpose is to create a mandate that will refocus attention on cognitive development and how trauma diverts the normal developmental process.

Contents

INTRODUCTION

Addiction: A Statement of the Problem

The hottest places in hell are reserved for those who, in
a period of moral crisis, maintain their neutrality.
—JOHN F. KENNEDY

Twenty-five percent of all annual deaths in the United States are from the use of tobacco,[2] alcohol,[3] and illicit drugs.[4] The federal government's conservative estimate is that over 623,000 addicts die annually from associated "diseases." That's six people every five minutes. , I think that meets the definition of a crisis. NIH, National Institute of Drug Abuse Revised May 2016[5]

What are the etiologies of these "diseases," and how are they treated? The agencies of the government that fund, study, and support the treatment of addictions *give a definitive answer.* The National Institute of Health's (NIH) is the parent organization for the National Institute of Alcohol Abuse and Addiction (NIAAA) and the National Institute on Drug Abuse (NIDA) and both list the definition of addiction as: Addiction is defined as a chronic, relapsing brain disease that is characterized by compulsive drug seeking and use, despite harmful consequences. It is considered a brain disease because drugs change the brain; they change the structure and how it works.[5] NIH lists genetic factors as probably the single most significant contributor to addictions suggesting that "as much as half of a person's risk of becoming addicted depends on his or her genetic makeup."[6] However, based on the concordance ratios of monozygotic- and dizygotic-twin studies performed an apparently contradictory conclusion is drawn. According to their research in the COGA project, "Although great progress is being made in the search for the genetic bases of the susceptibility for developing alcoholism, specific genes predisposing to alcohol use disorders have yet to be identified...Genetic models that postulate a single gene are not supported by the research results."[7] The American Society of Addictive Medicine (ASAM) continues to define it as a *chronic brain disease.*[8] To their credit, they have broadened the scope of their definition to be far more inclusive of social, psychological, learning, and biological factors, yet they still cling to the spiritual (or possibly moral) ones. Unfortunately, they also still cling to the approximately 50 percent contribution of genetics. Critical to the prevailing argument are the three necessary and sufficient conditions to make their case for a disease: a "hijacked brain," compulsive drug seeking, and self-harm. All three organizations agree in their support of the disease model of addiction and on a combined strategy of psychotropic antagonists, medication and psychological interventions for treatment. ASAM even recommends the twelve-step model as part of inpatient treatment modalities.

Some critics of the BDMA have attacked the model on the basis of the support the scientific evidence has provided and whether the promises for the efficacy of the social consequences proposed have actually occurred. They argue that: "the BDMA is not supported by animal and neuroimaging evidence to the extent its advocates suggest: it has not helped to deliver more effective treatments for addiction: and its effect on public policies toward drugs and people with addiction has been modest. The focus of the BDMA is on disordered neurobiology in a minority of severely addicted individuals, which undermines the implementation of effective and cost effective... " [94]

I am proposing that there is clinical and scientific evidence that there are more useful psychological models explaining more aspects of addiction than the BDMA which can lead to remediation of the disorder. I propose that there is more recent scientific information about the etiology of addiction that may provide both a more complete understanding of the disorder and evidence-based treatment that would necessitate a revision of the existing paradigm.

Consider the following points:

- The psychiatric community has replaced the terms *addict* and *addiction* with *substance use disorder* (SUD). This reduces any stigma attached to those who become dependent on opioid medications for pain management following medical procedures. I question this distinction; not all who are treated with opiates become addicted following medical procedures. What is the secondary gain? This is more of the "hijacked brain" model.

- The American Psychiatric Association (APA) believed that there was not sufficient empirical evidence of the effects of Adverse Childhood Experiences to include a diagnosis of a developmental trauma disorder in the *Diagnostic and Statistical Manual of Mental Disorders*, Fifth Edition. I find this irresponsible when the information from the epidemiological data provided by the Kaiser Permanente ACE Study conducted by Dr. Felitti and reported by Drs. Felitti and Anda—which had an incredible sample size of over 17,000—clearly demonstrated the effect of ACEs on the development of mental disorders.[9]

- I have used *addict, addiction,* and *SUD* as they are familiar terms with which we typically describe behaviors that people engage in. They are used in a non-pejorative sense.

- Antagonists are drugs that eliminate the *positive effects* of an altered state of mind. They eliminate the altered state. For example, antagonists like Naloxone block some of the receptor sights for opiates.

- Psychoactive substances are used to alter unpleasant states of mind (including boredom) or enhance positive states of mind. This is known as self-medicating.

- Drugs that are used as positive reinforcements (such as an R+ that reduces unpleasant mental states) lose their effect due to habituation. Habituation renders them ineffective at altering unpleasant states and enhancing pleasant ones; as a result, addicts must increase the amount consumed to produce the desired effect.

- Antagonists do not treat the underlying maladaptive psychological state that created the desire or perceived need to avoid experiencing that unpleasant maladaptive self-concept state.

- The approach of NIH is a combination of eliminating drug use, medications and cognitive behavioral therapy as the treatment options of choice. However, despite their recognition of factors other than biological ones, they have no mandate to explore other options that do not rely on *genetic* and *moral-weakness* hypotheses.

It is understandable that the intransigence of addiction has fostered and supported the belief that the only valid explanation is that addiction is a biological and probably genetic disorder. The most expensive scientific research into addiction is biological (e.g., neural imaging, psychopharmacological, and so on.). The final tally on that line of research is that we are not much closer to finding the "addictive gene" than we were when we started looking. We cannot find a cocktail of psychotropics that will cure addiction or even reliably mask its symptoms. Forty-odd genes "may be" contributors in some way. Neurobiology is clearing up some of the misconceptions of earlier research, such as the drug-usurpation hypothesis, which concluded that, once addicted, the brain has been unalterably changed both structurally and functionally. In other words, *once an addict, always an addict.*

There was contradictory evidence of this as early as 1940. In his study of morphine addiction in chimpanzees, D. Spragg demonstrated that they preferred a piece of fruit to morphine *except when they were in acute withdrawal.*[10] In 1991, M. A. Nader, who conducted a study on rhesus monkeys, demonstrated that increasing the amount and availability of a nondrug reinforcement made it preferable to cocaine.[11] Contemporary research continues to support findings that refute the drug-usurpation hypothesis, yet this information does not appear to be part of the dialogue designed to unravel the apparent anomalies of addiction. Is that because we don't or can't keep addicts in a cage and manipulate variables? Or is it because the decision about causation (a biological disease) has already been made—and once made, was forever set in stone?

The biological argument fails to find support when you examine the success of one its most influential opponents: Alcoholics Anonymous. With a combination of beliefs predicated on the disease model and non-biological/medicinal interventions, AA actually eschews the use of alcohol antagonists (e.g., naltrexone)[12] in favor of a *no-other-drugs* policy, despite their proven efficacy in supporting sobriety. In fact, AA utilizes behavioral, cognitive, and spiritual interventions to treat many addicts and alcoholics. Anne M. Fletcher estimates that 70 to 80 percent of all programs in the United States rely on AA as a primary treatment tool.[13] Many providers have little or no formal training other than what they received from successfully obtaining sobriety through AA and Narcotics Anonymous (NA). They still cling to the genetic hypothesis, which probably creates confusion about the genesis of addiction in those selecting AA/NA treatment. Unfortunately, there is not much data collected to validate their AA/NA claims of success.[14] These assessments of AA/NA will be reviewed in more detail shortly.

The assertion of the big three that addiction is a chronically relapsing brain disease with structural highjacking and compulsive drug seeking with self-harm can be questioned on other fronts as well. The reliance on early animal studies that demonstrated compulsive drug seeking were flawed on multiple methodological grounds and obviously ignored the frontal and prefrontal cortices of humans. The roles of comorbidity, neurobiology, learning, and trauma provide alternative plausible explanations of the intransigence of addictions.

I am proposing that it is time to critically evaluate our existing paradigm regarding addiction etiology and treatment that is over eighty years old. In order to create more effective treatment protocols, it is the purpose of this book to offer a multifaceted alternative explanation to the genetic-disorder hypothesis of the disease model. The data does not support the claim that we know enough about addiction to refuse to examine (let alone collaborate on) the real causes of addiction.

The crux of the problem has relied on the misperception and lack of understanding of the explanatory utility of *self-destructive behavior to the person exhibiting it*. This is a recurrent theme that will be addressed frequently, as self-destructive behavior is counterintuitive to those observing it. To both the trained and untrained eye, continuing to engage in behaviors that make your life unmanageable makes absolutely no sense. The hosts of ills that accompany addictions, in all their forms, are unfathomable to those who have not chosen to hurt themselves. They ask, "If poking yourself in the eye hurts, why would someone continue to poke him- or herself in the eye?" By dispensing with the genetic argument for a moment, we can begin to examine alternative hypotheses to what appears to be self-destructive behavior *to outside observers* (e.g., family, friends, and treating professionals). The alternative hypothesis will focus on learning theory; the relationships between learning, cognition, automatic brain functioning, emotion, early trauma, and cognitive development; and the role of language on our perception of reality.

> *Loyalty to petrified opinion never broke a chain*
> *nor freed a human soul—and never will.*
> —SAMUEL LANGHORNE CLEMENS

Nicotine, Alcohol, and Drugs (NADs)

NADs are psychoactive substances. It's a misnomer to define nicotine and alcohol as something other than drugs; they are, by definition, mind-altering drugs. Their legal status doesn't preclude the fact that they are psychoactive and prone to be addictive. They reliably change the way we feel; they dull, alter, enhance, or remove feelings we do not want, at least temporarily. Therein lies their utility to the user and the source for widespread use and addiction. The term *addiction* has been replaced in the *DSM-5* with the term *substance use disorder* (*SUD*) to discriminate between drug dependence following medical procedures—necessitating powerful analgesics that are primarily opiates and their derivatives—and what we once referred to as *addiction*, a term that has pejorative overtones.

Surgeon General Dr. Vivek Murthy was recently featured on national television, and he addressed the use of opioids for pain reduction as well as the observation that some individuals become addicted through opioid therapy for acute pain following medical procedures.[15] I do not question the results, but I do question the conclusion. If it's the drug, why doesn't everyone who is treated with opioids for pain become addicted to them? In a later recorded conference, Dr. Murthy reiterated the current paradigmatic view of addiction as a "chronic disease."[16]

There may be a small genetic compliment that is worth addressing, but it is neither the solution nor the substantive causal agent. There is no skin reaction, the hallmark of an *allergic response*, and no redness, rash, or itching, which are the signs and symptoms of an allergy. Severe allergies can lead to anaphylactic shock and death if left untreated. No such skin reactions accompany substance abuse. I've been assured by addicts of every age group that they do it because it makes them feel better. *Better* means *not like I was feeling before: mad, sad, glad, scared, or bored.*

Because the behavior makes no apparent sense to those outside of the addiction, the obvious mysteries of addiction (counterintuitive, self-destructive behavior) are what have led us to the search for a biological explanation. Working in a rehabilitation setting forced me to reexamine my beliefs about addiction as well as the contradictions inherent in the current dogma regarding addiction. Throughout my career, I believed that it was an *adaptive response* to psychological trauma. After I retired, I began volunteering at a treatment facility based on the AA/NA model. I was confronted, by both staff and residents, with the belief that addiction is a biological disorder or a "physical disease." This was confusing to me, as the residents had *voluntarily terminated* their use of their drug(s) of choice as this was a requirement for entry into the program. My response was to begin my search for the scientific validation of the disease hypothesis. Was addiction a chronic relapsing brain disease?

My own beliefs (or schemas) regarding addiction were tested and even assaulted when the residents of the rehab facility discovered that their disease had suddenly gone into spontaneous remission. Many had "reached their bottom" (a concept currently being challenged for its validity); they were medically injured or seriously ill, penniless, and living on the streets. Many were also facing unwanted legal sanctions. The "mysteries of rehab" actually supported my schema regarding the very nature of addiction. The assault on my addiction schema forced me to recognize that throughout my lengthy career of over forty years, I had dealt with only one kind of "tree" in the "addiction forest." I had thought I was looking at the rule rather than the exception to the rule. More questions were raised when I was confronted with the mysteries of rehab.

The Mysteries of Rehab

These are just a few of the mysteries that forced me to reexamine the validity of my closely held beliefs regarding addiction.

- The explanation that entering rehab can induce the spontaneous remission of a biological disease.
- Self-destructive behavior that violates the rules of behaviorism is exhibited.
- Early traumas are minimized and/or dismissed, as caregivers *did the best they could with what they had*. Justification applies to all early environmental influences, not just to the parents.
- Addiction is *not* viewed as destructive behavior targeting the self.
- Older addicts have lost their belief in their ability to change. They often say, "I am now, and forever will be, an addict and/or alcoholic."
- Despite the seriousness of addiction, accurate information about addiction is sorely lacking.
- The majority of the addicts in rehab were members of fringe groups (e.g., the stoners) in high school.
- Most addicts between eighteen and twenty-five years of age began their drug use when they were between twelve and fifteen. As such, one-third of their lives and their important cognitive-developmental stages were inhibited by drugs.[17]
- Most of the rehab residents have debilitating early maladaptive schemas (EMSs).[18]
- Addicts consistently cite an unwillingness to accept responsibility for their addiction. They feel justified by saying, "It's a biological disorder. How can you fix something that is completely beyond your control?"
- When addicts say, "I do fine when I'm in rehab," they mean, "I do fine when others (staff) monitor my behavior—when I turn over my executive power (frontal and/or prefrontal cortex) to them and they assume the *adult decision-making function* of my personality."

These are the issues that must be addressed if we are to make any progress in the treatment of addiction. After all, *a thinking disorder that precedes self-destructive behaviors produces 25 percent of all deaths each year.*

CHAPTER 1

New Science? New Paradigm? No!

What Does the Epidemiological Research Tell Us about the "Trees" in the "Addiction Forest"?

Approximately 6–10 percent of the population of the United States (or twenty-two million people) are estimated to experience problems with substance abuse or dependence. The American Psychiatric Association (APA) altered the official APA nomenclature in their *Diagnostic and Statistical Manual of Mental Disorders*, Fifth Edition (DSM-5)[19] from *addiction* to *substance use disorder* (SUD) and removed the multiaxial diagnostic system to integrate with the International Classification of Disease System (ICD), which is transitioning from ICD 9 to ICD 10.

The National Epidemiological Survey and Related Conditions (NESARC) surveyed more than forty-three thousand individuals who are representative of the US population, using questions based on the *DSM-4's* criteria for alcohol abuse and/or dependence. Their findings led them to the startling conclusion that alcoholism isn't what it used to be.[20] Some of their findings are as follows:

- Many heavy drinkers do not have alcohol dependence (AD); of those who consume five or more drinks daily, only 7 percent develop dependence.
- Most develop only a mild to moderate disorder in which they primarily experience impaired control. They do not exhibit health, social, vocational, or legal problems.
- About 70 percent of affected persons have a single episode that lasts four years. It appears there are two types of alcohol dependence: *time limited* and *recurrent/chronic*.

- Twenty years after the onset of alcohol dependence, about three-fourths of affected individuals are in full recovery; more than half of those who have fully recovered drink at low-risk levels without any symptoms of alcohol dependence.
  - Author's insert: I do not recommend that those of you who have exhibited the recurrent/chronic version of AD interpret this finding as permission for you to try controlled drinking—*that's too much like playing Russian roulette!* The sections on learning and neural plasticity will explain why.
- About 75 percent of persons who recover from *time-limited* alcohol dependence do so without seeking any kind of help, including from specialty alcohol programs (rehab) and AA. Only 13 percent of people with diagnosable alcohol dependence ever receive specialty alcohol treatment, and it is estimated that 80–90 percent of rehabs are based on the AA model.

"These and other recent findings turn on its head much of what we thought we knew about alcoholism," Dr. Mark Willenbring, director of the NIAAA's Division of Treatment and Recovery Research wrote. "As is often true in medicine, researchers have studied patients seen in hospitals and clinics most extensively. This can greatly skew understanding of a disorder, especially in the alcohol field, where most people neither seek nor receive treatment and those who seek it do so well into the course of the disease."

I hope it is obvious at this point that the attributes of the "trees" (individuals with recurrent/chronic AD) have served to define the attributes of the "forest" (individuals with time-limited AD), or the majority of alcohol-consuming individuals. If that is correct, these phenomena are considered to be statistical *outliers* and are furthermore described as a "clinician's illusion,"[21] which is often the result when you use data from a clinical population to describe an entire population. Outliers may actually indicate by their very intransigence that they are not part of the main group but represent a subgroup. When it is necessary to delineate the defining characteristics of the group in question (chronic, relapsing, compulsive-drug-seeking, brain-diseased individuals), the finding is that the majority of the drinking population does not represent recurrent/chronic AD individuals (the outliers). Therefore, the recurrent/chronic AD population represents the exception, not the rule. Is there another reasonable explanation for the problems experienced by the outliers?

Comorbid Disorders and SUDs

Co-occurring/comorbid disorders with SUDs may broaden our understanding of the re-current/chronic subpopulation. One of the most important variables in understanding the relationship between comorbid disorders and successful treatment is the relationship between outcome predictors and successful treatment. D. A. Ciraulo et al. report that

> the following factors have been identified consistently: severity of dependence or withdrawal; *psychiatric comorbidity*; substance-related problems; motivation (abstinence commitment); length of treatment; *negative affective states; cognitive factors; personality traits and disorders; coping skills*; multiple substance abuse; contingency contracting or coercion; genetic factors; sleep architecture; urges and craving; *self-efficacy*; and *economic and social factors*. Although it is well known that severity dependence (including polysubstance abuse), *serious psychiatric comorbidity*, and *social problems* are associated with *poor treatment response*, only recently has research examined the efficacy of intervention strategies that specifically address these problems. *Adequate treatment of psychiatric comorbidity and improvement in social, economic, and family functioning lead to better treatment outcomes*...With some exceptions, *identification of biologic predictors has not led to innovative therapies*. One of these exceptions is the development of naltrexone for the treatment of alcoholism, which was based in a solid theoretical rationale and followed by hypothesis-driven experiments.[22]

J. P. Smith et al. explored a gap in the literature regarding the relationship between generalized anxiety disorder (GAD) and individuals seeking outpatient SUD treatment and concluded that

> of thirty-nine outpatients meeting criteria for an AUD [alcohol use disorder], nearly half (46 percent) also met criteria for current GAD. The onset of GAD occurred prior to AUD in 67 percent of comorbid cases, with an average time lag of 12.5 years among individuals with primary GAD. Participants with comorbid GAD-AUD endorsed higher levels of worry severity and worry-reduction alcohol expectancies, and 56 percent of comorbid participants had a history of suicide attempts...Study findings provide initial evidence that GAD may be a prevalent and relevant factor among individuals with AUD seeking outpatient substance-abuse treatment.[23]

Like S. B. Quello et al. did in their aricle,[24] they cited S. H. Stewart and P. J. Conrod's review of available empirical literature,[25] which reported that 75 percent of anxiety disorders precede an SUD—a finding they posit supports the *self-medication hypothesis*.

Quello et al. reported that "mood disorders, including depression and bipolar disorders, are the most common psychiatric comorbidities among patients with substance use disorders. Treating patients' co-occurring mood disorders may reduce their substance craving and taking and enhance their overall outcomes." They also stated that the relationship between mood disorders and SUDs has been a topic of concern for the last twenty-six years, what with empirical data establishing the nature of this relationship in the National Institute of Mental Epidemiological Catchment Area's (ECA) study,[26] conducted in the 1980s, and the National Comorbidity Survey (NCS) conducted in 1991.[27] Both provided striking documentation that mood disorders increase the risk of SUD. In the ECA study of individuals with a mood disorder, for instance, 32 percent had a co-occurring SUD; of individuals with lifetime depression, 16.5 percent had an alcohol-use disorder and 18 percent had a drug-use disorder. SUDs were particularly common among individuals with bipolar disorder; 56 percent had a lifetime SUD. Citing the findings of the NCS conducted in 1997,[28] they reported that, "compared with individuals with no mood disorders, those with depression were approximately twice as likely, and those with bipolar disorder approximately seven times as likely, to have an SUD."

They also cited M. G. Kushner et al.'s literary review,[29] which reported that—per the recent review of the available empirical literature—anxiety disorders predate substance-use disorders in at least 75 percent of cases, thus further supporting the increased prevalence of the *self-medication pathway* compared to alternative mechanisms. This lends further credence to Kushner's earlier findings on the relationship between alcohol problems and anxiety disorders.[30]

The data on the co-occurrence of other mental disorders with SUDs may allow us to explain the discrepancies in the data created by the outliers. The director of the NIDA, Dr. Nora D. Volkow, reports the following:

The high prevalence of this comorbidity has been documented in multiple national population surveys since the 1980s. Data show[s] that *persons diagnosed with mood or anxiety disorders are about twice as likely to suffer also from a drug use disorder (abuse or dependence) compared with respondents in general. The same is true for those diagnosed with an antisocial syndrome such as antisocial personality or conduct disorder. Similarly, persons diagnosed with drug disorders are roughly twice as likely to suffer also from mood and anxiety disorders...*

Further, *males are more likely to suffer from antisocial personality disorder,* while *women have higher rates of mood and anxiety disorders, all of which are risk features for substance abuse...Finally, because more than 40 percent of the cigarettes smoked in this country are smoked by individuals with a psychiatric disorder,* such as *major depressive disorder, alcoholism, posttraumatic stress disorder (PTSD), schizophrenia,* or *bipolar disorder, smoking by patients with mental illness contributes greatly to their increased morbidity and mortality.*[31]

Schizophrenics are not the main topic of this book, but their predilection for nicotine adds credence to the self-medication hypothesis. As the same report says, "the rate of smoking in patients with schizophrenia has ranged as high as 90 percent. Nicotine or smoking behavior may also help people with schizophrenia deal with the anxiety and social stigma of their disease."

What Do We Know about the Etiology of Mental Disorders?

Most mental disorders are created primarily by exposure to traumatic events and environments during early developmental periods. They develop when the world that children are exposed to is chaotic; dangerous; stressful; devoid of affection; or physically, psychologically, emotionally, or sexually abusive. They can come from a lack of attention, parental disinterest, drug abuse, poverty, unpredictability, minority status, and so on. Persistent domestic violence, the death or major illness of a caregiver, and divorce can all precipitate PTSD. However, PTSD is not limited to childhood; it can be caused by traumatic events at any age. These chaotic, unpredictable childhood environments create what Jeffery Young defines as early maladaptive schemas (EMSs), which are conclusions children draw from *their interpretation* of what the world is like and what their place in the world is. These schemas are based on their perception of the treatment they have received. Of course, individual temperamental differences can contribute to an inaccurate perception of self.

Others have described these traumatic childhood issues as adverse childhood experiences (ACEs), primary contributors to SUDs. They cite statistically reliable data demonstrating the strong relationships between ACEs and the proclivity for SUDs. Maia Szalavitz, for instance, cited a study of the entire Swedish population: "Even just one extreme adversity—like losing a parent or witnessing domestic violence—before age fifteen doubles the odds of substance use disorders." She concluded that "the strong dose/response relationship between the amount of traumatic experiences [ACEs] a person has and his or her risk for addiction is undeniable."[32]

The data the Center for Disease Control (CDC) collected from an ACE study[33] consisted of information from seventeen thousand participants in ongoing health screenings who had discussed the number of ACEs they had been exposed to. The findings from this and other studies regarding ACEs will be discussed later, in the section on trauma. Suffice it to say, the findings support the data presented regarding early-childhood traumatic environments and mental disorders producing difficulties in adjustment from almost the inception of the ACEs.

So, what is the etiology of mental disorders? The *DSM-5* provides information on the antecedent conditions in its descriptions of family-of-origin characteristics that produce mental disorders. In each of the comorbid disorders' descriptions of the antecedent conditions, family-of-origin issues figure prominently and include a variety of maladaptive rearing environments, such as those consisting of physical, psychological, and/or sexual abuse; abandonment; and/or parental impairment (e.g., AD and/or SUD, poverty, ethnicity, adoption, observation of violence, domestic violence, the death of a parent, a divorce, etc.). The major co-occurring disorders that precede SUDs are presented for the corroboration of the salient early environments that produce EMSs, are the potential precursors of, and are highly correlated with subsequent addiction.

From the previous discussion, it is clear that other mood and behavioral mental disorders comorbid with AD and/or SUDs typically precede AD and/or SUDs. Is it possible that substance use is not a primary causal agent but instead an attempt to treat the primary mental disorder by altering the way the user feels? Is this supportive of the self-medicating alternative? When we examine the antecedent conditions such as disorders of mood, affect, personality and behavioral disorders, we find traumatic early environments are typical antecedents. What does the *DSM-5* report regarding antecedents? In the interest of brevity, I have included only the relevant temperamental, environmental, genetic, risk and prognosis, and comorbidity comments.

Depressive Disorders
Risk and Prognostic Factors

- Temperamental: neuroticism (negative affectivity) is a well-established risk factor for the onset of major depressive disorder, and high levels appear to render individuals more likely to develop depressive episodes in response to stressful life events.

- Environmental: adverse childhood experiences, particularly where there are multiple experiences of diverse types, constitute a set of potent risk factors for major depressive disorder. Stressful life events are well recognized as precipitants of major depressive episodes, but the presence or absence of adverse life events near the onset of episodes does not appear to provide a useful guide to prognosis or treatment selection.

Anxiety Disorders
Specific Phobia Risk and Prognostic Factors

- Temperamental: temperamental risk factors for specific phobia, such as negative affectivity (neuroticism) or behavioral inhibition, are risk factors for other anxiety disorders as well.
- Environmental: environmental risk factors for specific phobia, such as parental overprotectiveness, parental loss and separation, and physical and sexual abuse, tend to predict other anxiety disorders as well. As noted earlier, negative or traumatic encounters with feared objects or situations sometimes (but not always) precede the development of specific phobia.

Panic Disorder

- Environmental: reports of childhood experiences of sexual and physical abuse are more common in panic disorder than in certain other anxiety disorders. Smoking is a risk factor for panic attacks and panic disorder. Most individuals report identifiable stressors in the months before their first panic attack (e.g., interpersonal stressors and stressors related to physical well-being, such as negative experiences with illicit or prescription drugs, disease, or death in the family).

Agoraphobia

- Environmental: negative events in childhood (e.g., separation, death of parent and of parents, and other stressful events, such as being attacked or mugged, are associated with the onset of agoraphobia. Furthermore, individuals with agoraphobia described the family climate and childrearing behavior as being characterized by reduced warmth and increased overprotection.

Generalized Anxiety Disorder

- Comorbidity: individuals whose presentation meets criteria for generalized anxiety disorder are likely to have met, or currently meet, criteria for other anxiety and unipolar depressive disorders. The neuroticism or emotional lability that underpins the pattern of comorbidity is associated with temperamental antecedents and genetic and environmental risk factors shared between these disorders, although independent pathways are also possible. Comorbidity with substance-use, conduct, psychotic, neurodevelopmental, and neurocognitive disorders are less common.

Obsessive-Compulsive Disorder (OCD)

- Temperamental: greater internalizing symptoms, higher negative emotionality, and behavioral inhibition in childhood are possible temperamental risk factors.
- Environmental: physical and sexual abuse in childhood and other stressful or traumatic events have been associated with an increased risk for developing OCD. Some children may develop the sudden onset of obsessive-compulsive symptoms, which has been associated with different environmental factors, including various infectious agents and postinfectious autoimmune syndrome.
- Genetic and physiological: the rate of OCD among first-degree relatives of adults with OCD is approximately two times that of first-degree relatives of adults without the disorder; however, among first-degree relatives of individuals who had an onset of OCD in childhood or adolescence, the rate is increased tenfold. Familial transmission is due in part to genetic factors (e.g., a concordance rate of 0.57 for monozygotic versus 0.22 for dizygotic twins) and of parents. Dysfunctions in the orbital frontal cortex, interior cingulate cortex, and stratum have been most strongly implicated.

Trauma and Stressor-Related Disorders

Risk and prognostic factors are generally divided into pretraumatic, peritraumatic, and posttraumatic factors.

Pretraumatic Factors

- Temperamental: these include childhood emotional problems by age six (e.g., prior traumatic exposure, externalizing or anxiety problems and parent and prior mental disorders (e.g., panic disorder, depressive disorder, PTSD, or OCD).
- Environmental: these conditions include a lower socioeconomic status; lower education; exposure to prior trauma (especially during childhood); childhood adversity (e.g., economic deprivation, family dysfunction, or parental separation or death); cultural characteristics (e.g., fatalistic or self-blaming coping strategies); lower intelligence; minority racial/ethnic status; and a family psychiatric history. Social support prior to the event exposure is protective.
- Genetic and physiological: for adults, these include being of female gender and a younger age at the time of trauma exposure. Certain genotypes may either be protective or increased risk of PTSD after exposure to traumatic events.

Peritraumatic Factors

- Environmental: these include severity (dose) of the trauma (the greater the magnitude of trauma, the greater the likelihood of PTSD); perceived life threat; personal injury; interpersonal violence (particularly trauma perpetrated by a caregiver or witnessing a threat to a caregiver); and, for military personnel, being a perpetrator, witnessing atrocities, or killing the enemy. Finally, dissociation that occurs during the trauma and persists afterward is a risk factor.

Posttraumatic Factors

- Temperamental: these include negative appraisals, inappropriate coping strategies, and development of acute stress disorder.

- Environmental: these include subsequent exposure to repeated upsetting reminders, subsequent adverse life events, and financial or other trauma-related losses. Social support (including family stability, for children) is a protective factor that moderates outcome after trauma.

Comorbidity

Individuals with PTSD are 80 percent more likely than those without PTSD to have symptoms that meet diagnostic criteria for at least one other mental disorder (e.g., depressive, bipolar, anxiety, or substance-use disorders). Comorbid substance abuse disorder and conduct disorder are more common among males than among females. Among US military personnel and combat veterans who have been deployed in recent wars in Afghanistan and Iraq, co-occurrence of PTSD and mild Traumatic Brain Injury TBI is 48 percent. Although most young children with PTSD also have at least one other diagnosis, the patterns of comorbidity are different than in adults, with oppositional defiant disorder and separation anxiety disorder predominating. Finally, there is considerable comorbidity between PTSD and neurocognitive disorder and some overlapping symptoms between these disorders.

Personality Disorders

When discussing *personality disorders*, the *DSM-5* describes the following level of personality functioning:

> Like most human tendencies, personality function is distributed on a continuum. Central to functioning and adaptation are individuals' characteristic ways of thinking about and understanding themselves and their interactions with others. An optimally functioning individual has a complex, fully elaborated, and well-integrated psychological world that includes a mostly positive, volitional, and adaptive self-concept; a rich, broad, and appropriately regulated emotional life; and the capacity to behave as a productive member of society with reciprocal and fulfilling interpersonal relationships. At the opposite end of the continuum, an individual with severe personality pathology has an impoverished, disorganized, and/or conflicted psychological world that includes a weak, unclear, and maladaptive self-concept; a propensity to negative, dysregulated emotions, and a deficient capacity for adaptive interpersonal functioning and social behavior.

Disruptive, Impulse-Control, and Conduct Disorders

The disruptive, impulse-control, and conduct disorders have been linked to a common externalizing spectrum associated with the personality dimensions labeled as *disinhibition* and (inversely) *constraint* and, to a lesser extent, negative emotionality. The shared personality dimensions could account for the high level of comorbidity among these disorders and their frequent comorbidity with substance-use disorders and antisocial personality disorder. However, the specific nature of the shared diathesis that constitutes the externalizing spectrum remains unknown.

Oppositional Defiant Disorder

- Temperamental: temperamental factors related to problems in emotional regulation (e.g., high levels of emotional reactivity or poor frustration tolerance) have been predictive of the disorder.
- Environmental: harsh, inconsistent, or neglectful childrearing practices are common in families that include children and adolescents with oppositional defiant disorder, and these parenting practices play an important role in many causal theories of the disorder.

Intermittent Explosive Disorder

Risk and Prognostic Factors

Environmental: individuals with a history of enduring physical and emotional trauma during their first two decades of life are at increased risk for intermittent explosive disorder.

Conduct Disorder

- Temperamental: temperamental risk factors include a difficult, uncontrolled infant temperament and lower-than-average intelligence, particularly with regard to verbal IQ.
- Environmental: family level risk factors include parental rejection and neglect, inconsistent childrearing practices, harsh discipline, physical or sexual

abuse, a lack of supervision and early institutional living, a frequent change of caregiver, a large family size, parental criminality, and certain kinds of familial psychopathology (e.g., substance related disorders). Community level risk factors include peer rejection, association with a delinquent peer group, and neighborhood exposure to violence. Both types of risk factor tend to be more common and severe among individuals with the childhood-onset subtype of conduct disorder.

- Genetic and physiological: conduct disorder is influenced by both genetic and environmental factors; the risk is increased in children with a biological or adoptive parent or sibling with conduct disorder. The disorder also appears to be more common in children of biological parents with severe alcohol use disorder, depressive or bipolar disorders, or schizophrenia or biological parents who have a history of ADHD or conduct disorder. Family history particularly characterizes individuals with the childhood-onset subtype of conduct disorder.

- Comorbidity: ADHD and oppositional defiant disorder are both common in individuals with conduct disorder, and this comorbid presentation predicts worse outcomes. Individuals who show the personality features associated with antisocial personality disorder often violate the basic rights of others or violate major age-appropriate societal norms, and as a result, their pattern of behavior often meets criteria for conduct disorder. Conduct disorder may also co-occur with one or more of the following mental disorders: specific learning disorder, anxiety disorders, depressive or bipolar disorders, and substance-related disorders.

What Does the Data Support?

This data and the data that follows have been presented to support the premise that there is a causal relationship between what a child experiences in his or her early environment and that child's subsequent addiction. It is very difficult to discount the contribution of early developmental environments, especially when the data suggests that it may be the mental disorder of the parent that fosters the development of the disorder in the child. The status quo has been that the chemical imbalance causing the mental disorder in the offspring is transferred genetically. Hence, a standard question used during a mental-health interview is, "Has anyone in your family had any mental disorders?" This query is directed at determining whether the current disorder was inherited. In psychological circles, we have recognized that these negative transgenerational processes are simply learned behaviors developed and supported by a person's environment: "We only buy Fords." "All of my family members are Republicans." "There is one true God, and his name is—"

The burgeoning field of epigenetics has already demonstrated that the manifestation of a specific gene caused by environmental factors can be lost in subsequent generations. The marvelous adaptability of organism's never ceases to amaze me. Advances in epigenetics will hopefully add to our understanding of how the nature versus nurture controversy can be appropriately conjoined.

An "Owner's Manual" for Addiction

To reiterate, this book has been written with multiple purposes in mind:

- It is my contention that the unyielding focus on the search for the roots of the biological disorder—the *disease model*—has misdirected our ability to accurately assess the etiology of this disorder for too many years.
- The intransigence of addictive behavior was considered proof positive of its being a biological disorder; this has misdirected our attention for the last eight decades. The statistical *outliers* defined the population of occasional and recreational psychotropic-substance users.
- The disproportionately high death rate of the SUD population (25 percent of all deaths annually) is accounted for by the fact that they have not been accurately diagnosed by the current treatment zeitgeist and have not received the appropriate "medicine" for their disorder.
- Unfortunately, the population of outliers' self-destructive behavior defined addiction, which led to inadequate diagnosis and inappropriate treatment.
- Ignoring the rules of behaviorism allowed treating professionals to ignore the fact that the self-destructive behavior had both positive and negative reinforcing values for those individuals exhibiting the behavior.
- Given what we know about co-occurring mental disorders it is imperative to ask, "Who should be treating what?"

Most importantly, this book has been written to draw attention to the temperamental and environmental conditions that predispose a child to SUDs—to establish the viability of the effects of the conclusions that a child derives about him- or herself by being exposed to *adverse childhood experiences* that lead to *early maladaptive schemas* and other *comorbid disorders*.

To that end, I want to state categorically that *I do not care how you get well but only that you do get well*. If the treatment strategy you have been using isn't working, ask yourself these questions:

- "Have I been accurately diagnosed for recurrent/chronic versus time-limited AD, a comorbid disorder, or PTSD?"
- "Am I doing my part in treatment?"
- "Is my therapist or sponsor doing his or her part?"
- "If I'm not getting better is it because I have selected a treatment product that is not suited to my condition and, have I been informed that there other options?"

If you are an alcoholic, check with a medical professional in case you require medical detox. Regardless of your drug of choice, if you are ready to quit, consult a medical professional regarding the safest way to terminate your use.

I'm tired of hearing that "*relapse is a part of recovery* and *progress, not perfection*. Yes, relapse can be a part of recovery, but it is not a requirement! *Progress, not perfection* can be a rationalization for your saying, "I've got one more run in me" or "I can control it now" or "I'm not ready to address the issues that drive the behavior or don't know what they are." Be careful what you argue for!

Help is available, for those of you exhibiting high-risk behaviors that could develop into addiction, *to remind you that that nicotine, alcohol, and illicit drugs account for 25 percent of all deaths that occur in the United States annually—and that those with SUDs represent only about 10 percent of the population.*[34]

To the treating professionals, including AA and NA practitioners who follow the prevailing paradigm of addiction being a biological disease—which has guided our attempts at intervention for over eighty-one years—I would remind you that this modality has not produced results, even at chance levels. Death-by-addiction numbers have not decreased! To that end, I would ask each treating professional to do some *reality testing* on the efficacy of the model you are currently using. This reality testing requires you to ask yourself at least the following two questions:

- "Do my patients/clients remain clean and sober following the interventions I employ?"
- "Does the environment I am working in provide adequate follow-up and support, which is critical to post treatment success?"

If the answer is no (or even a resounding no), I hope the hypotheses I offer in the following chapters will add to your repertoire of intervention strategies. I'm not suggesting that what I offer is the *only* way; rather, I offer it as *another* way.

Reality Testing: Who Are We Talking About?

I doubt seriously that anyone in active addiction will be reading this book. The *demand characteristics* of addiction require that the addict's attention is directed singularly at *avoiding withdrawal*. The clinical training I received taught me that attempting to make a *contract for treatment* with someone who is in a drug-induced altered state is a waste of time. Also, we do not allow minors to enter into contracts because we know that they do not fully understand either the responsibilities or the consequences of their commitment.

The data on *state-dependent learning* reminds us that something learned in an altered state is completely available only in that altered state. Professionals in the field know that there is a period of time following the cessation of the use of mind-altering substances during which the chemistry of the brain has to be recalibrated. During this process, the brain struggles to begin its natural production of the neurotransmitters that the substance abuser has been disrupting with illicit chemicals designed to occupy the same receptor sites. At this time, the cognitive processes involved in learning, understanding, and memory can be impaired, from mildly to severely. This is not to suggest that someone who is abusing drugs or alcohol cannot quit cold turkey and remain sober; many out there have done so. However, medical detox is recommended for those who have been maintaining high levels of alcohol or other drugs in their system. When in doubt, consult a physician.

This book provides information primarily for those who may have attempted a treatment strategy many times and failed to make any improvement. Much of the lore about addiction suggests that you must "reach your bottom" before you seek treatment; therefore, if treatment fails, it is because "you did not really reach your bottom." This is a marvelously circular argument, which places 100 percent of the responsibility for treatment failure on your shoulders and moreover vindicates the treating professionals for "your failure." Maia Szalavitz, who struggled with this aspect of her own recovery, addresses and effectively debunks this notion in her book *Unbroken Brain: A Revolutionary New Way of Understanding Addiction*. I will directly address the issue in Chapter 5 on learning theory.

Could you be an *outlier* who did not receive appropriate treatment rather than someone who is *constitutionally incapable of being rigorously honest*? One of the jokes I learned early in my career as a psychologist is as follows:

Question: "How many psychologists does it take to change a lightbulb?"
Answer: "Only one—but the lightbulb must be willing."

This joke, on many levels, is a reminder to treating professionals, lay treatment providers, and addicts alike. First, regardless of how many reinforcers you think you control as a treating professional, the person you are dealing with will always have the option to refuse to respond to them. For instance, during World War II, some Jews chose death over collaboration, meaning that they voluntarily forfeited their lives in order to remain firm in their belief that refusing to cooperate with the enemy was the right thing to do. (This is not an indictment of those who did not.) Second, if you, an addict, are seeking treatment to please others, your investment in success is limited. Third, one of the most successful treatments for addiction relies on a *contractual agreement* between you, the patient/client, and the treating professional. Only then will you have decided that you *want* or perhaps *need treatment* because it will have become a matter of life or death for you. A contractual agreement is one of the cornerstones of cognitive behavioral therapy (CBT).

The fact that your very real and serious desperation drove you to seek treatment means that you finally did *accurate reality testing of your own situation*. What will become clear in this book is that I do not blame you for treating professional's failure to provide the best evidence-based treatment to successfully treat you. If you are reading this book, what is abundantly clear to me is that you are no longer discounting:

- that you have a problem;
- that it is a serious problem;
- that it is a solvable problem; and
- most importantly, *that you have the ability to solve it.*

You have humbled yourself and admitted that you did not know how to solve the problem. And so, you have come to the professional and/or spiritual community for assistance. It is my professional opinion that your decision to seek treatment *places the ball squarely in the treating professional's court.*

Sponsors, whether you recognize it or not, you are taking on the responsibility of a treating professional. Your "sponsees" operate from the premise that if you have obtained a year of sobriety, you are competent (*you have the professional expertise*) to teach them how to obtain and sustain their sobriety. Your limited training may come only from how you completed your step work and whatever you may have learned about addictive (self-destructive) human behavior during your own addiction. Is it also possible that you were a *time-limited* rather than a *recurrent/chronic* type? If you were a *time-limited* type, do you have the skills to understand (let alone treat) a *chronic/recurrent* type? Did you even know there was a difference between the two?

Central to the treatment paradigm I am proposing is the premise that hurting yourself serves a purpose for you. This will make more sense when you read the sections on trauma, early maladaptive schemas, and learning theory that discuss how and why such behavior is maintained. To those of you who have made the commitment to obtain treatment, I strongly recommend that you obtain as much "clean time" as possible before you begin the arduous task of figuring out why you have been hurting yourself. This clean time will allow your brain to recalibrate so that you can fully participate in your recovery. Some data suggests a minimum of three months. Of course, treating professionals created twenty-eight-day programs when they assumed that it took an addict a week to detox, a week to begin thinking straight, and a couple of weeks to practice staying abstinent.

I congratulate you on your decision to stop hurting yourself and your willingness to give up your *self-destructive behavior*. Once again, the notion that *you are hurting yourself* is critical to this treatment philosophy and method; it is the only thing that makes any sense when you take all that we know into account.

Most of you, regardless of your formal educational level, are very intelligent and capable of grasping everything I have presented; therefore, I have not dumbed anything down. (If you have questions about anything I've written, visit my website, dockennethwilson.com, and I will do my best to answer them.) What you have taught me, and what I have observed, is that if we give you the knowledge of *what your addiction really is*—and, most importantly, *where it comes from*—you will have increased the number of tools that you have to use for your recovery. The likelihood that you will remain clean and sober also increases dramatically. The purpose of this book is to add tools to your recovery toolbox and turn you into an informed consumer of addiction-treatment products. The ability to fix something that is broken or malfunctioning is based on having *an accurate understanding of how it was designed to work and what might have broken it.*

Of course, *we are talking specifically about the outlier part of the addicted population.* The time limited members of the substance use population usually quit using inappropriately between 25 to 30 years of age. Coincidentally, this is the age when the prefrontal cortex (or decision-making function) has reached full maturity. Most of those who once used excessively are able to do accurate reality testing on their drinking when they are faced with adverse environmental consequences (e.g., a DUI, warnings from work, spousal or other familial disapproval, their first blackout, and/or an unfavorable liver panel), which convinces them that their substance use is sufficiently disruptive to their life. With that epiphany, they curb their behavior without any further legal, medical, or societal interventions.

The individuals at this end of the continuum are capable of doing accurate reality testing; they recognize that their behavior is self-destructive, and they make the decision to stop it. They have determined that they want a manageable lifestyle. When they are queried about this change in their behavior, they respond by saying, "It wasn't working for me, so I stopped." I should add that this is not the population I am presenting or representing here. My primary contact has been with those who are severely addicted and have extensive histories of substance abuse, typically beginning in their early teens. They have chosen or at least accepted treatment as an alternative to incarceration, longer programs, or therapeutic communities. I have spent the last twenty-five years of my career with patients reporting the following histories. I am not speaking to recreational users of mind-altering substances. However, if your "recreational use" is creating *problems in your life*, then this is for you: *denial is not just a river in Egypt.*

The severely addicted are presenting for treatment from late adolescence through their sixties. When addicts do accurate reality testing on their use histories, many realize that they have overdosed a number of times and simply accepted that they have a disease over which they can have no control. Because of their number of failed attempts at sobriety, they have reached the point where they're actually trying to kill themselves because they see no other way out of their addiction. I frequently hear, "This is my last chance. If I don't understand why I'm still an addict now, I'll die." Many even vividly describe their failed attempts at suicide—their multiple overdoses and weapons of choice—and quite typically detail the quantity of alcohol or other drugs they consumed to produce their own death (BAC levels above 0.3, 0.4, and 0.5). Some come for treatment because they have been given the medical diagnosis that their body can't take any more of this abuse. Others come because they have given up on their ability to change their behavior—and this may be their fifth or sixth attempt at rehab. They have reached the *I'm-helpless-and-it's-hopeless* state; desperation has set in.

Most of the older patients and an alarmingly large number of the younger patients have lost all hope; they've lost everything and everyone. They've become homeless. Some have been rejected by their families. Many have been divorced one or more times, had social services take their children, or given their children up in the belief that those children would be better off without them. Many have also accumulated multiple DUIs, misdemeanor and felony convictions that result in incarceration and are seen as the high cost of illicit drug use. Many have stolen, "slung drugs," or even become commercial sex workers to support their habits and have thus courted serious legal consequences. Many are so desperate that in their heart of hearts they truly believe this is their last chance at treatment, and if they don't succeed this time, they might as well use until they die—the sooner, the better.

When they tell their stories, the majority confess to having had a traumatic child-hood that has so far gone untreated. If in AA, they believe that their lack of willpower or their diseased, genetically defective brain is the cause of their addiction, not just a symptom. How often do I hear them say, "I was sexually abused, and my parents didn't believe me and even punished me for lying"? Those who present with undiagnosed or untreated comorbid disorders comprise at least 90 percent of the population I typically see in my practice.

The good news is that I know thousands with these historical antecedents who are leading successful lives after having been given the tools to understand what their addiction really is, where it comes from, and how they can make peace with their original demons. These demons—*trauma-induced early maladaptive schemas and harmful scripts*—suggested that self-destruction was their best option. Fortunately, any new demons that they've created in service of their self-destructive behavior are treatable. There is hope!

I once mentored an IV drug user at the Salvation Army's VIPER Program in Sarasota, Florida. This is a multifaceted program that operates philosophically from an AA base. I admired their work so much that, a year or so later, I volunteered my services to the community recovery program (CRP) at the same facility. I have to thank the Salvation Army's City of Hope in Sarasota, Florida,[35] for allowing me to do this. It was there that I was confronted with the *disease model* with so much ferocity that I had to question my own schema regarding the causes of addiction. I had never before worked in an AA treatment environment or treated addiction as a morally deficient or biological disorder—even though I fully understood the relationship between observable behavior and the underlying physiological substrate.

Of equal importance in understanding addiction is the relationship between the psychotropics that the addicts and/or alcoholics have been self-administering and the ones that occur naturally in the brain in service of self-medication.

I've always viewed addictions as symptoms, not the cause, of a treatable psychiatric disorder that is usually precipitated by some traumatic etiology. I know personality disorders frequently develop and possibly co-occur as a consequence of the behaviors required to support addictions.

It is vitally important to differentiate between the two conditions (time-limited and chronic/intermittent) in making treatment decisions. Why? In 1996, the NIAAA stated that the "single confirmed match reported today is between patients with low psychiatric severity and twelve-step facilitation therapy."[36] Such patients had more abstinent days than those treated with cognitive-behavioral therapy.

By the time the *chronic/intermittent* types reach treatment, they are usually diagnosed with multiple mental disorders. While the SUD may be the presenting symptom secondary diagnostic conditions may include any of the following; a personality disorder, a mood disorder, PTSD, anxiety, and ADD or ADHD. According to Elizabeth Nosen et al., mood disorders are also typically comorbid with this population.[38] They studied the relationship between PTSD cues and AD cues and found that the highest craving was elicited when these cues were paired and when alcohol-dependent individuals experienced an increase in their feelings of guilt, anxiety, and fear.

The residents who are admitted to the Salvation Army's City of Hope CRP must be clean and sober upon entry (i.e., they have not tested positive for chemicals of abuse). They may have been so for a matter of days or a matter of months or anything in between. Remember, what struck me was that it made no sense for spontaneous remission to happen to so many patients at the same time, or that so many of them would fall out of remission at the same time after having left treatment. I had always worked in long-term programs and had never witnessed this phenomenon. This very vigorous assault on my addiction schema forced me to investigate the validity of my own beliefs; thus began my search for scientific evidence that would either support or oppose the disease model that the staff and residents clung to so strongly.

The Search for New Data

In mid-2015, during my search for empirical data, serendipity brought new information to my attention. Deidre Tygart CAC III, one of the substance-abuse counselors from the Stout Street Foundation who I helped to train, alerted me to a *Huffington Post* article. It provided me a broader perspective regarding both addiction and recovery. The article was about Johann Hari's *Chasing the Scream: The First and Last Days of the War on Drugs*.[37] This book was first presented in January 2015 but was updated on May 5, 2015.

I checked several of the studies Hari cited but especially Dr. Bruce Alexander's Rat Park study,[38] with which I was unfamiliar. The Rat Park experiments studied rats that had been addicted for sixty-five days. When taken out of the addicting environment of a solitary cage and reunited with their cohorts in an enriched environment, the rats either eased off their quest for the drug-laced water they had been given instead of plain water or quit it entirely. How can this be if their brains had been hijacked?

L. Robins et al.'s article on heroin-addicted Vietnam returnees cited the unexpected finding that 90–95 percent of the servicemen gave up the use of heroin upon returning home, with or without treatment.[39] Most of those who persisted to use had been addicted before they served.

Neither of these studies nor their observations support the concept of a "hijacked brain," which has been the cornerstone of the biological disease paradigm. Both citations were from peer-reviewed journals and appeared to have been properly reported. Of course, I had previously examined Virginia Davis et al.'s article on the effect of tetrahydroisoquinoline (THIQ) on rat brains,[40] which has been misreported and misrepresented by several sources. These purportedly credible sources erroneously stated that when Davis was studying "winos," she had an epiphany while discussing her findings with ER staff. This never happened, yet many "reputable" treatment facilities still report that it did.

In my earlier efforts to find support for the disease model, I had come across the HAMS Network, which questions several of the myths about addiction.[41] The group, whose name stands for *harm reduction, abstinence, and moderation support,* also disseminate information regarding addiction. After reading entries on that website I decided to reexamine the monozygotic-twin studies. I was particularly interested in those who were reared apart as that would support the nurture rather than nature position. I found that the study demonstrated limited support for heritability among female twins; proportionately, yet females are more prone to abuse alcohol for the purposes of self-medication than men. Perhaps it is the social acceptability of alcohol over *drugs?*

L. Bevilacqua and D. Goldman, who are strongly committed to the heritability hypothesis wrote, "Although use of addictive agents is volitional, addiction leads to loss of volitional control."[42] This is the "hijacked-brain" hypothesis, cleverly cloaked by the changes in brain structure that follow a period of addiction. "These neuroadaptive changes are key elements in relapse." In direct contradiction, they then—in citing K. S. Kendler et al.'s article[43]—noted that "the Virginia Twin Study revealed that in early adolescence the initiation and use of nicotine, alcohol, and cannabis are *more strongly determined by familial and social factors*, but these gradually decline in importance during the progression to young and middle adulthood, when the effects of genetic factors become maximal, declining somewhat with aging." There is no mention, in this description, of the relevant psychological factors created in the family of origin or of the environmental influences, such as trauma or EMSs, which are demonstrated antecedent factors that lead to the self-medication associated with substance use during adolescence.

In my opinion, the accumulation of data that contradicts the prevailing hypothesis that addiction is a chronically relapsing brain disease requires that we, as treating professionals or consumers of addiction products, reexamine our schemas regarding the causes of and treatments for addictions.

Relapse as a Validation of the Disease Model

I am not arguing that relapse doesn't occur; I am arguing that the existing attribution—that relapse is the function of a "hijacked brain"—is invalid. A memory trace (the synaptic pathway of a behavior that has been practiced thousands of times) creates a well-traveled neural super-pathway that is likely to be repeated when the eliciting cues are available. That's what learning is all about.

If the brain has been hijacked and there is no volition available, how then does the substance abuser voluntarily cease drug use to enter rehabilitation facilities?

The following paragraphs will present empirically validated scientific data that confirms the availability of more plausible—and therefore more viable—non-biological treatment options. I am not arguing against antagonists that reduce or eliminate the effects of the drugs of choice of SUD patients; in truth, I support them. They can be critical for some in early recovery for the prevention of relapse, as they eliminate the psychological relief of trauma-related psychological pain, sought through the drugs of choice), and support abstinence. When addicts were offered naloxone for free, they were unwilling to accept it. I would hypothesize that their reluctance to do so was related to the fact that the negative affective states were not alleviated by the antagonist. In other words, the drug did not resolve the problem.

What Does the Elephant Look Like?

Consider the parable of the six blind men who were asked to touch an elephant and describe what it looked like. They were unable to come to a consensus because they each touched a different part (leg, tail, trunk, etc.) and could describe only that one part; none could see the big picture but only what limited data was available to them. Fortunately, that is not the case with the sources I am about to present, all of which describe different aspects of what we call addiction. We all agree it is not a chronically relapsing brain disease. In fact, the following books and articles are offered for your consideration so that you can determine the validity of that belief.

If you are data driven and wish to read up on some of the peer-reviewed research that has emboldened me to present an alternative hypothesis to the prevailing biological model of addiction, I urge you to use the following reading list. Each of the sources listed below sheds light on an aspect that provides a comprehensive, contrarian view of the current objections to the disease model.

- *Chasing the Scream: The First and Last Days of the War on Drugs*, by Johann Hari.
    - The bibliography is extensive and will lead you in many directions. Hari discusses the historical antecedents of the United States's war on drugs, geopolitical consequences of the war, governmental interference with physician medical treatment, and humanitarian treatment of addiction in other countries. It is an excellent overview.
- *The Rise and Fall of the Official View of Addiction*, by Bruce K. Alexander.
    - This and other articles and speeches can be accessed on his website.[44]
- Bruce Alexander's Rat Park experiments and his refutation of the current chronically relapsing brain-disease model.
    - In the 1970s, the early research he and his colleagues conducted refuted the "hijacked-brain" data that fueled the beliefs about what addiction really was.
- Dr. Jeffery Young's work on early maladaptive schemas.[45]
    - His is an empirical analysis of the beliefs about how one's sense of self can result in pathological self-destructive behaviors. Young presents the ways in which these internal belief systems develop and how they are maintained, and he offers CBT for their treatment.
- S. H. Ahmed et al.'s "Neurobiology of Addiction versus Drug Use Driven by Lack of a Choice."[46]
    - This research demonstrates that the cornerstone experiments establishing the "hijacked-brain" hypothesis were flawed and drew an inappropriate conclusion from their results. They demonstrated that when nondrug options were available, rats would choose a nondrug option.

- *The Sober Truth: Debunking the Bad Science Behind Twelve-Step Programs and the Rehab Industry*, by Dr. Lance Dodes and Zachary Dodes.[47]
  - Dodes and son spend the first fifty-seven pages examining the available information that supports the lack of efficacy of AA treatment.
- *The False Gospel of Alcoholics Anonymous*, by Gabrielle Glaser.[48]
  - She presents an overview on the current relevant issues of addiction and the lack of empirical support for AA treatment.
- *Inside Rehab: The Surprising Truth about Addiction Treatment—And How to Get Help That Works*, by Anne M. Fletcher.
  - Fletcher has conducted an extensive review of what actually goes on in most "rehab" facilities and how little theorists know about that which is being offered as effective treatment.
- L. Robins et al.'s "Narcotic Use in Southeast Asia and Afterwards."[49]
  - This follow-up on the heroin-addicted servicemen who stopped using following their return from Vietnam has been included because it was so difficult to find and, though discussed, it is seldom cited.
- *Unbroken Brain: A Revolutionary New Way of Understanding Addiction*, by Maia Szalavitz.
  - This book presents extensive data on the causal relationship between adverse childhood experiences and subsequent addictive behavior. Szalavitz addresses temperamental, environmental, learning, and epigenetic findings, in addition to brain structure and function, to support her assertions.
- *The Body Keeps the Score*, by Bessel van der Kolk.[50]
  - This author puts his thirty years of studying trauma and PTSD to work with a bio-psycho-physiological compendium of data, which includes information on the neural and physiological responses to stress and trauma.

What's at Stake?

Does One Size Fit All?

It is important to understand that there is a continuum of what we call addiction. First, the data indicates that many who drink excessively acknowledge that they have a problem and stop using on their own. Another subset of the population includes those who are defined as functional alcoholics/addicts; they use excessively but still continue to function and don't make a shambles of the world around them. There are also binge drinkers and weekend drug users—those who consume substances excessively but only occasionally. Further up the scale are those who engage in risky behaviors, such as driving while under the influence, and learn their lesson after one DUI, or suffer the consequences of a minor drug offense and don't continue to use. On the other hand, there are those with multiple DUIs, who have become far more injurious to the general public and themselves. Finally, there are illicit drug users whose addiction has increased to the point that they are engaging in illegal behaviors in service of their addiction. The latter two categories have typically suffered severe and life-threatening physiological symptoms (including, but not limited to, damage to their liver, heart, and lungs and hepatitis B and C) or numerous blackouts, overdoses, and near-death experiences. They have attempted multiple programs and still find themselves unable to curb their self-destructive behavior.

Those of us who work in the business are fully aware that this continuum exists. We know that AA's "one-size-fits-all treatment" is a dangerous fantasy. It is irresponsible to be ignorant of the limits of your skill set; understanding the limits of what you have the ability to do can be critical to the health of those seeking the only treatment they may be aware of, too much is at stake! As licensed professionals, we are specifically forbidden to attempt treatment in any area in which we have not been trained and demonstrated competence. Violation of this provision can result in anything from a reprimand to suspension or even revocation of one's license to practice. Who do sponsees complain to if they think their sponsor (1) was uninformed about an aspect of their addiction, (2) attempted or refused to treat something he or she knew nothing about, or (3) failed to acknowledge that there are other options?

If you are an AA advocate or sponsor, don't stop reading! I am not advocating for the elimination of AA; I am only suggesting that you could use some continuing education, as most mental-health professionals are required to obtain annually. After all, whether you admit it or not, you are practicing psychotherapy and behavior modification without a license. You *assume* the model works if you are/were, or a sponsee is/was, successful, but you also relegate your sponsees' failures to (1) their unwillingness to change, (2) the belief that they haven't really "reached the bottom,"

(3) their constitutional inability to change, or (4) their inability or unwillingness to faithfully follow AA principles. For instance, chapter 5 of *The Big Book* states, "Rarely have we seen a person fail who has thoroughly followed our path. Those who do not recover are people who cannot or will not completely give themselves to this simple program, usually men and women who are constitutionally incapable of being honest with themselves. They are not at fault; they are born that way. They are naturally incapable of grasping and developing a manner of living which demands rigorous honesty."[51]

Is it possible that those AA considers the "constitutionally incapable" are our outliers—those with predisposing mental diagnoses who require some form of treatment before they can obtain sobriety?

If you are an AA sponsee, has the organization informed you or even suggested that there may be two basically different populations out there who require diverse treatments for their dual diagnoses?

When you distill the premise of AA, a member's failure to obtain sobriety is the result of multiple personal failures, such as having a weak will or a constitutional inability/congenital defect or lacking the ability to be honest with him- or herself. So, if you start AA and relapse, it is not a failure of an attempted intervention but a mental and/or moral defect on your part. We call this process blaming the victim. It's not too encouraging to your integrity and self-concept, but it certainly is an incentive for you to acknowledge that you need a higher power to help you conquer this (what AA and NA both consider to be a) disease.

Assuming that Anne Fletcher's *Inside Rehab* is correct, since AA and NA receive 70–80 percent of the patient load by default, you sponsors should have the best skill set to make therapeutic and triage decisions. You should therefore also be able to answer the following:

- Which treatment modality is most successful with a particular set of presenting symptoms?
- Does AA believe (either explicitly or implicitly) that all addictions will respond to AA treatment, regardless of type or etiology?
- Is there a comorbid disorder (e.g., depression, anxiety, personality disorder, or drug-induced psychosis) that should be addressed first, or in conjunction with the addiction, or treated with referred for adjunctive medication?

Do Any Empirical Assessments Suggest What the Most Effective Treatments for Addiction Are?

The Building Recovery by Improving Goals, Habits, and Thoughts (BRIGHT) Study[52] found significant differences between experimental and control groups. Patients with SUDs and co-occurring depression were randomly assigned to one of two groups; one group were given usual care while the other were given usual care plus CBT. Their findings stated this:

> On the depression-symptom instrument used in the study, at three months, patients receiving the intervention [usual care plus CBT] generally had mild symptoms and patients receiving usual care alone generally had moderate symptoms. At three months, 55.8 percent of patients in the BRIGHT group had minimal symptoms, compared with 33.6 percent in the control group; at six months, these numbers increased to 63.9 percent and 43.8 percent respectively. Among patients no longer living in a treatment center at the six-month mark, those in the intervention group had fewer days of problem substance abuse and fewer drinking days than did those in the usual care group.

Like it or not, we are all in the business of treating a psychiatric rather than a primarily biological disorder. There is no question that disulfiram, acamprosate, naloxone, and other opioid antagonists promote abstinence and sobriety, yet AA/NA do not promote them. Why not? Cessation of the psychological pain associated with trauma is achieved as psychoactive drugs take effect. Psychological relief is the reinforcement produced by a long chain of *operant behaviors*. One of the best ways to terminate an operant sequence is to eliminate the payoff. Drugs that are antagonistic to opiate and other receptors weaken the relationship between what you do and what you get out of it; they provide only temporary symptomatic relief.[53]

The question then becomes, is adhering to dogma more important than offering another proven and well-documented aid to sobriety?" Adherence to dogma is not sobriety. I am obligated to notify my patients that they are welcome to obtain a second opinion.

One of the few studies that met the criteria of a scientifically controlled experiment looked at the effectiveness of different treatment modalities on workers who had been referred for treatment because their alcohol consumption was interfering with their job performance.[54] Their behaviors had come to the attention of their supervisors, who had then referred them to the Employee Assistance Program (EAP). Dr. Diana Walsh et al. excluded those workers who required medical detox at the time of admission as their BAC levels were 0.20 or higher. The 227 who did take part in the study were randomly assigned to one of three groups. Seventy-three were assigned compulsory hospitalization plus one year of probation and mandatory AA attendance at least three times per week. Eighty-three were assigned compulsory AA attendance only and were offered an escort to a local meeting, which they were advised to continue attending (daily if possible, but no less than three times a week for at least a year). The seventy-one patients assigned to the third group were given a choice of treatments: of those patients, twenty-nine elected hospitalization; thirty-three went directly to AA; three chose outpatient psychotherapy with psychiatric social workers or marriage counselors; and six opted for no organized help at all. Data was collected at intervals: one, three, six, twelve, eighteen, and twenty-four months later.

The data indicated—unexpectedly—that the group who had been assigned compulsory hospitalization plus probation and mandatory AA attendance was the most successful; the group who had been given a choice of treatments found moderate success, and those who had been assigned compulsory AA attendance only were the least successful in terms of their continued alcohol abuse. I would hope that being made aware of the scientific attempts to make sense out of the very complex problem of substance abuse would suggest taking a closer look at our beliefs regarding substance-use disorders. A thorough review of the study's pros and cons concerning AA's efficacy as a treatment modality can be found in the two meta-analyses of studies that meet the scientific criteria for inclusion.

In *Alcoholics Anonymous Effectiveness: Faith Meets Science*, Dr. Lee Ann Kaskutas describes a technique called "meta-analysis," with which inclusive criteria are developed to establish the necessary conditions to claim causation rather than correlation. She found that "the experimental evidence for AA effectiveness (addressing specificity) is the weakest among the six criteria considered crucial for establishing causation."[55] In *correlation*, things that occur together are assumed to be caused by one of the conditions. Say you believe the superstition that warns, "Step on a crack, break your mother's back." If you stepped on a crack and your mother's back was broken, you would assume that stepping on the crack was what caused the injury. *Causation* is established when you eliminate as many competing variables or conditions as possible and can then demonstrate that A caused B. If you can reliably demonstrate that you can walk a straight line, touch a finger to your nose with your eyes closed, and stand on one foot when there is no alcohol in your system but are unable to do so when your BAC level is 0.20 or higher, we have established a causal relationship between high concentrations of alcohol in your system and your ability to perform simple motor tasks. That's *causation*.

The Cochrane Database of Systematic Reviews is acknowledged as the most rigorous database for presenting the results of scientific data. Its findings are included in Kaskutas analysis. However, empirical support for the efficacy of AA/NA is rather more difficult to find. The unwillingness of AA/NA to perform scientifically appropriate studies makes it difficult to establish the efficacy of twelve-step treatment. I suspect much of the confounding results is related to attempting to treat a subpopulation of outliers—the *chronic/intermittent*—which reduces the successful outcomes attributable to AA and confounds the data's results. *AA outperformed CBT only in the population with low psychiatric comorbidity and only in a single study, which has not been replicated.*

I know a large number of persons who attribute their sobriety to their continued participation in AA. There is no question that it works for a segment of the population, but they are not the focus of this book.

AA adherents, you have shared your knowledge with me, and now I would like to share mine with you. Unfortunately, the current "hijacked-brain" *disease model* will not change with this book; that will take many more years and the accumulation of much more scientific data. We all need to recognize that the existing schema regarding addiction is antiquated and actually quite dangerous when you consider what is really at stake: the lives of addicts and those closest to them. In the meantime, millions will suffer and/or die from the ravages of addiction. Almost any average citizen I could talk to would tell me that addiction is a disease; it is the prevailing view. Unfortunately, the disease model is well entrenched in our belief system. That said, cessation of the destruction caused by addiction may just motivate you to consider the possible validity of the paradigm shift I am proposing.

A reminder: if you haven't yet read Johann Hari's *Chasing the Scream*, I suggest that you do so. It is replete with articles and data from other countries as well as other methods for treating addiction that appear to be far more successful than our current war on drugs and disease model. Hari presents data on crime rates before and after prohibition, and there certainly is no doubt about the proliferation of drug cartels created by the criminalization of mind-altering substances. He also discusses alternative treatment methods, in which attitudes toward addiction are less fraught with moral overtones.

This '70s Rat Park experiment offered a rat in isolation the choice between drugged water and non-drugged water. The reliably recurrent outcome was that the rat would choose the drugged water. What this finding did was cement in our minds, and the minds of those in treatment and scientific communities, that *the drug* "hijacked" *the brain*. That is, volition was lost, and substance use was no longer an act of will as the "choice- decision making" part of the brain was eliminated. The rats would repeatedly press a bar to receive a dose of morphine, even neglecting to eat, sometimes until they died.

Compulsive Drug Seeking and the "Hijacked Brain"

The term *hijacked* is attributed to Bill Moyers, who, in a 1998 PBS television series on addiction, cited the work of Alan I. Leshner: "Scientific advances over the past twenty years have shown that drug addiction is a chronic, relapsing disease that results from the prolonged effects of drugs on the brain."[56] Leshner further stated that; "recognizing addiction as a chronic, relapsing brain disorder characterized by compulsive drug seeking and use can impact society's overall health and social policy strategies and diminish the health and social costs associated with drug abuse and addiction."

The Oxford Dictionary defines compulsion as "an irresistible urge to behave in a certain way, especially against one's conscious wishes." With compulsion, the *biological/brain* overcomes the *cognition/mind,* eliminating the *choice* function of the frontal and prefrontal cortices. This process will become more clear when we learn to discriminate between the brain and the mind, hardware and software.

In 1998, G. M. Heyman was one of the first psychologists to object to the notion that addiction is a *compulsion.* He cited epidemiological research, which shows that "addiction is the psychiatric disorder with the highest recovery rates and the shortest duration. Experimental and clinical studies show that the factors that influence voluntary behavior, such as economic and social costs, persuade many addicts to quit using drugs. Not mentioned is the fact that voluntary behavior is mediated by the mind, conscious awareness, and the extensive findings on relapse rates and recovery."[57] He further noted that the addicted population who do present for treatment have *a 60–70 percent comorbidity rate* while the population of those who stopped using without treatment have *a comorbidity of around 30 percent,* comparable to the rates of the general population. A reasonable conclusion to draw from this data is that comorbid disorders are an impediment to responding to the common social cues and constraints and the normal cognitive and motivational factors mediating intensive, long-term addiction.

Heyman revisited the issue in 2013, after the accumulation of fifteen more years' worth of data. In "Addiction and Choice: Theory and New Data," he stated that "the relevant research shows most of those who meet the American Psychiatric Association's criteria for addiction quit using illegal drugs by about age thirty, that they usually quit without professional help, and that the correlates of quitting include legal concerns, economic pressures, and the desire for respect, particularly from their family members. That is, the correlates of quitting are the correlates of choice, not compulsion."[58]

Is There an Alternative Explanation?

Bruce Alexander's work on drug addiction was prompted when he asked this question: "Is there anything unique about the defining addiction experiment that studies lone rats in isolation?" What he found was that the addiction he had observed in the original experiment was what science defines as an *artifact of the experimental design*. These were not rats in a normal environment with multiple choices but ones confined in a cage with an unpleasant environment, devoid of companionship. Dr. Alexander wanted to test the null hypothesis that regardless of the environment a rat was in, it would continue to drink drugged water because its brain had been hijacked. The alternative hypothesis was that access to a normal environment would allow the rat to stop behaving like an addict.

Dr. Alexander was able to demonstrate that rats who had been addicted for sixty-five days, when placed in a rat-friendly environment, either stopped drinking the drugged water or reduced their consumption of it significantly. This kind of experiment strikes right at the heart of the belief that drugs *hijack the brain*, and that *once the hijacking has occurred, you are addicted for life.*

Neurobiologists have recently been cautioning their researchers to be aware of any artifacts in experiments that include an *addiction option* but no competing *non-addiction option*. In their article entitled "Neurobiology of Addiction versus Drug Use Driven by a Lack of Choice," Serge H. Ahmed et al. cogently argued that the defining experiments that solidified our belief in the "hijacked-brain" theory were based on a lack of choice—and he cited Bruce Alexander's Rat Park experiment. I think this is an accurate but erroneous interpretation of the data. In scientific terms, this is an artifact. Yes, the rats did become addicted and preferred the drugged water over nondrugged water, but their *environment* was a definitive factor in the "choice" at hand. *Choice can make the difference.*

Ideally, this test could be achieved by reconstructing in the laboratory a small version of the real world, as Dr. Alexander did for his experiment. In Rat Park, rats lived together in a large enriched colony that offered several different behavioral options, including taking morphine orally from a drinking bottle. When compared to rats living alone in a standard housing cage, the rats living in Rat Park drank much less morphine. This outcome shows that the ability to engage in other activities during drug access, including social interactions, can prevent drug use in most rats. *This is another finding that challenges the drug-usurpation hypothesis of addiction.*

Ahmed et al. further stated they "encourage neurobiologists involved in addiction research to increase animals' choice during drug access, preferably by supplying alternative rewarding pursuits."

In the early to mid-1930s, the adoption of the biological model of addiction was not only reinforced but embraced because the scientific and medical communities could offer no viable alternative.

AA has been the major player in addiction treatment since the mid-1930s. Those in charge of the war on drugs discouraged any medical alternatives, and so, AA became the treatment of choice by default. Johan Hari provides ample data on how, in the early days of the war on drugs, the government discouraged physicians' attempts to treat addiction as a medical problem. Psychology and psychiatry were still in their infancy and didn't have viable constructs to offer as an alternative. According to the Oxford Group, addiction was a moral failing prompted by personal problems of fear and selfishness that required "moral rearmament." Today, we have new scientific data that indicates there are viable alternatives to our antiquated view of the nature of addictions and their treatment.

I'm not arguing that there is a conspiracy to maintain a schema about drugs and substance abuse; that is inaccurate. Neither am I arguing that there is malicious intent in our current attempts to make sense out of something that apparently does not make any sense: self-harm. What I am arguing is that when the accepted cause of a problem has been believed for fifty to seventy-five years, it is difficult for new data to find a sympathetic ear and make its way into the present-day zeitgeist. Remember that it requires energy to abandon a long-lasting schema, so any new data will frequently be identified as either an anomaly or incorrect.

The government has not focused on the antecedent conditions that lead to addiction, or on more effective treatment strategies, because our leaders have believed that the cause was already known and that the lack of successful treatment was validation for the disease model of addiction. When you already know the answer, there is no reason to ask the question.

As an academician, scientist, and psychotherapist, I am familiar with how funding works the kind of inquiries that are supported with grant money from funding agencies, and the accountability requirements that accompany the granting process. Funding agencies decide which research to support based in part on the schemas of those people who must decide which appears to be an investment that will advance our overall knowledge. The belief that we are dealing with a medical disease is held by the heads of the governmental agencies responsible for deciding which scientific directions to pursue. If they believe that it is an incurable biological disease, then their research dollars are sure to go to those who agree and continue to pursue the biological precursors to substance abuse and addiction. Incidentally, academia is a "publish-or-perish" environment, where tenure and advancement are primarily associated with publication. The overbearing need to constantly obtain grants to support your research is a burden. There is also the issue of the administrative overhead built into the grant, which goes to support faculty, grad students, and so on.

Unfortunately, the voices who suggest that the biological-disease model is impoverished and has not produced reliable decreases in substance abuse are few and far between and have basically been ignored. Bruce Alexander provided data that reliably demonstrated how a rat heavily addicted to drugs, if given the choice, would decrease or terminate its drug use when provided an environment conducive to non-drug-seeking behavior. After five years of experiments, the university he was teaching at discontinued the funding of his research; that was forty years ago. How did this incredibly valuable information regarding addiction fall on deaf ears?

Two very prestigious scientific journals—*Science* and *Nature*—deemed the research not worth publishing. Why? The peer reviewers must have either determined that the methodology was flawed or disagreed with the premise that drugs do not "hijack the brain" because it did not agree with their own addiction schema—which, incidentally, had been created by AA in the 1930s and had never been seriously questioned. The disease model has been the zeitgeist ever since. Dr. Alexanders' group had to publish their findings in a psychopharmacological journal, one that is not widely read by those involved in addiction theory or treatment. Their information did not reach their intended audience, who could have incorporated it into practice for thirty-five years. Sadly, during that same time, countless lives were lost and resources wasted.

For thousands of years, we humans believed that the Earth was flat, so nobody would sail their ship to where they knew they would fall off the edge of the world. Therein resides the power of belief systems. Remember that the concept of flying was inexplicable until the Wright brothers successfully challenged the existing belief system.

Glossary

Compulsion: an uncontrollable performance of an act

Contract for treatment: an agreement between a person presenting for therapy and a therapist that regards how a particular problem area will be treated in the duties and responsibilities of both participants

Demand characteristics: the focus placed on responding to the biological need to avoid withdrawal

Discounting: a way to avoid dealing with a particular problem by discounting the following facts:

- that a problem exists
- that it is a serious problem
- that it is solvable
- that you have the ability to solve it

Disease model: the belief that addiction is a biological disorder created by the chemical hijacking or usurpation of the brain, resulting in a chronically relapsing brain disease

Early maladaptive schemas (EMSs): self-destructive belief systems developed in childhood that limit a person's success

Harmful scripts: life plans that guide behavior in self-destructive ways

"Hijacked brain": an irreparable change in the structure and functioning of the brain caused by repeated substance abuse

Outliers: groups of subjects who *apparently* represent a population but don't

"Reach your bottom": used to describe the point at which substance abusers become so desperate that they turn to others for help

Reality testing: the ability to assess any given situation with an uncontaminated adult ego state (see the chapter on transactional analysis)

State-dependent learning: refers to the biochemical and psychological mental state that someone is in when he or she learns new information; students who load up on caffeine and cram before a test will better recall the information with a similar amount of caffeine in their system

Withdrawal: a physiological response in which the body reacts to the increasing absence of its psychoactive substance of choice

Zeitgeist: the defining spirit or mood of a particular period in history, demonstrated by the accepted facts and beliefs of the time

The Current Paradigm

Contemporary Theoretical Understanding of Addiction: Causes and Treatment

Addiction treatment in the United States is currently and primarily limited to two explanatory systems. The predominant system, which has been in place for seventy-six years, is the Alcoholics Anonymous model. The basic premise of the model was taken from the Oxford Group in England, who followed an Evangelical Christian model. The scarcity of scientific information at that time led to the conclusion that alcoholism was an incurable disease and that sobriety could be maintained only through an acknowledgment of your powerlessness and a reliance on a higher power (as you understood it) in addition to continued participation in the AA community. This works very well in a small, tightly knit community where members are not separated by space. There were no cell phones to use to call your sponsor, so face-to-face contact was primary. This "real community" can be an important element in recovery. The secondary system is also a biological model. The official stance of the medical (and, to some extent, psychological) community is that addiction is the product of a chronically relapsing brain disease. Much of the research has focused on brain imaging, psychopharmacology, and the neuroanatomical description of the loci in the brain involved in the brain's reward system(s).

These approaches are interesting but primarily descriptive, not explanatory. Philosophically, trying to explain something that occurs at the observable behavioral level at the neurophysiological level is called reductionism. What has been and is now being relegated to unreliable science is the contribution that contemporary cognitive and behavioral psychology can offer to understanding and treating debilitating behaviors.

Cognitive structures—*schemas*—are our facts and belief systems, and they are as valid, observable, and demonstrable as any other aspect of addiction that we can examine. Schemas are acquired through our interaction with the *unique* world that each and every one of us was raised in. This includes monozygotic twins; despite their identical DNA, through their subtly and not-so-subtly different environmental exposures, their experiences of the world are unique, or else they would also be behavioral clones. Most healthy schemas are useful and help us to navigate through a very complex world. Some schemas are maladaptive and may in part explain the self-destructive behaviors associated with addictions—that is, those behaviors that seem both counterintuitive and incomprehensible to those who don't possess maladaptive schemas.

Why would a normal, intelligent person continue to engage in self-destructive behaviors? A thorough understanding of *trauma* and how it manifests in maladaptive schemas may provide a more plausible explanation than the biological model does. Taking a drink, snorting, or ingesting/injecting psychotropic substances *all require an act of volition*. Maladaptive schemas, created by real or perceived trauma (perception is reality), provide an explanation as to why a person would exhibit *self-destructive behavior*. Biology, the principles of learning, and the physiology and psychology of habituation all help to make sense out of why the addictive behaviors are not easily terminated. The mind and brain in concert is what allows these acts to be committed. As the brain habituates to the current dose, that dose no longer blocks the unpleasant affective state and the brain signals the mind I need more. The process is not appreciably different than when you are thirsty and drink until your hypothalamus signals full. However, water is necessary to survival and another dose of ones drug of choice is a choice not related to survival. The unpleasantness of withdrawal is what makes the choice feel necessary.

The Significance of Schemas, Their Exceptions, and Their Anomalies—What Are Yours?

Schemas are our *personal* facts, not *the* facts. Are Fords really better than Chevrolets? Our belief systems regarding addiction are, in fact, *schemas*. They are beliefs about what addiction is, what causes it, and how it is to be treated. Unfortunately, one of the most important aspects of our schemas is that once they are created, they tend to self-perpetuate. What that means is that any information that is contradictory to one of our schemas has to be excluded or explained away, or it will force us to redefine the core beliefs at the center of that schema. It is far easier to consider any such information an anomaly or exception to the rule. Indeed, we develop schemas to eliminate the need to constantly evaluate our behavior and what we think we understand so that we can respond efficiently or even *automatically*. The alternative is "paralysis by analysis." What is your schema regarding addiction?

It is critical to understand that, regardless of how you think humans got to be humans, the primary function of the *brain* is to sustain, prolong, and perpetuate life. The *mind*, on the other hand, does not necessarily agree with the brain, and for reasons unknown, the *mind* will behave in ways that seem both counterintuitive and incomprehensible. Thus, a good share of this book will focus on possible reasons why the *mind* will contradict the *brain* and behave self-destructively.

All life forms either adapt to accommodate changing environmental conditions or die. It is my hope that regardless of your philosophical orientation, whether it is intelligent design or Darwinian evolution, we all learn to accept and acknowledge the fact that, at the very least, *some* organisms do evolve. I can think of two obvious examples that make this point. First, we had to develop a new rat poison specifically designed for rats because they evolved to become resistant to warfarin, the blood thinner we had previously used to kill them. Second, the *Staphylococcus aureus* (a bacterium) that lives in hospitals and that we once attempted to eradicate with various forms of antibiotics e.g., methicillin, has evolved into a form that is now methicillin resistant (MRSA)—an excellent reason to avoid hospitals. The most recent development in the evolution of *Staphylococcus aureus* is that there are now strains outside of hospitals that are similarly resistant to the antibiotics we have at our disposal. In my mind, an organism that cannot adapt to change has *a truly poor design, predicated on the belief that environments are immutable.* Therefore, it is my hope that you will read the information I have to offer with an open mind and not dismiss it because it may violate some or all of your core beliefs about addictions and/or our ability to adapt. Remember, we once believed that the Earth was flat, the planets revolved around the Earth, and bleeding was the way to cure diseases.

The broad topics we will be covering include the brain, the mind, learning, language, neurotransmitters/basic psychopharmacology, cognitive behavioral treatment options, the contribution of trauma to the development of maladaptive schemas, and the concept of subpersonalities/transactional analysis.

I would ask that you do not formulate objections to what I am proposing as regards addiction until you have finished absorbing all of the information here presented. I am offering what I have learned from addicts, which also happens to be supported by reliable science. Your current points of view regarding genetics, the disease model, psychological antecedents, the role of the brain versus the mind, and the necessity of relapse (among other things) may make this a difficult read already without your im-mediately offering any objections to a *schema* that is different from your own.

Your *addiction schema* is based on your combined system of information—the facts, opinions, and beliefs you currently hold on the subject of addiction. Everything you believe about causation, treatment, relapses, and the possibility of a cure will con-trol how you, as an addict, respond to treating your addiction or what you, as a thera-pist, will offer to your patients or clients. And so, this book is intended for multiple audiences—for addicts and gatekeepers alike, including those who study addiction, dictate what therapies are acceptable and will be paid for, and who will provide treat-ment for addicts.

Central to the paradigm I am proposing are these three pragmatic absolutes or assumptions that we must agree upon:

- Living organisms wish to live.
- All behavior has a purpose.
- Reinforcements—the positive, neutral, or negative outcomes of our behav-iors—are *idiosyncratically* defined. (See page 71 for more.)

CHAPTER 2

New Science

Rationalism: Programming the Human Bio computer; How Do the Brain and Mind Work?

The most interesting thing in my world is the human brain. The complex thinking, abstract reasoning, imagination, and overall creativity we are capable of represent only some of the cognitive skills that separate us from the rest of the animal kingdom. The way human intelligence develops and operates is both the blessing and bane of our existence. One blessing has been our ability to understand the physical world in such a way as to create technology that allows us to travel to the moon and back and view galaxies millions of light-years away. Conversely, that same technology allows us to allocate our resources in counterproductive ways, wage wars, rape the planet, poison its oceans, and accept that other members of the human race must starve. When we understand that we can warp the positive normal development of the brain, we will need to create a manual for child rearing and abandon the belief that anyone with a reproductive system has the inalienable right to reproduce.

What we've learned about the development and operation of the mind has been the *raison d'être* for psychological science. Our knowledge of the operation of the mind has progressed from the intervention of multiple deities; through the humors of earth, air, fire, and water; and through phrenology and homunculi, to our current knowledge of an electrical-chemical storage unit where information can be stored, processed, and manipulated. For a more complete understanding of the operation of human thinking as the precursor to human behavior, we will begin late in the game with the work of René Descartes, skip lightly over Frederick Bartlett's, Jean Piaget's, George Kelly's, and Aaron Beck's, and finally focus on that of B.F. Skinner and Jeffery Young.

When we use the term *brain*, we inadvertently ignore the fact that there is an unconscious part of the brain that works primarily without any conscious input on our part. What we usually mean when we say *brain* is the conscious, aware part of it, which is more correctly or effectively referred to as our *mind*. What is the difference? Of the approximately 86 billion cells in the brain cavity, approximately 16.9 billion are allocated for what we understand as consciousness or awareness. This includes those mental processes related to our perceptions, our learning, the recognition of our feeling states, our information processing, our language, and—most importantly—our *decisions* about which behaviors we can submit to and which ones we need to suppress.

One of the ways to think about this dichotomy is to use the metaphor of a computer. Computer hardware is what most of us don't understand; it's what they call machine language. The binary code (zeros and ones) is what allows the computer to perform its operations. The part we do understand is called software.

Descartes: Thinking, Observing, and Knowing

What is software, and where does it come from?

> *Dubito ergo cogito; cogito ergo sum.*
> *(I doubt, therefore I think; I think, therefore I am.)*
> —RENE DESCARTES, SEVENTEENTH-CENTURY SCIENTIST,
> MATHEMATICIAN, AND PHILOSOPHER

I agree with Descartes in principle; the fact that we can think about ourselves establishes our existence—"I think, therefore I am." Implicit in that statement, and every bit as important, is that we must also understand this:

> *Quis ego reputo sum est quis ego sum.*
> *(What I think I am is what I am.)*
> —KENNETH G. WILSON, PhD, TWENTY-FIRST-CENTURY PSYCHOLOGIST

The correlates of that assertion are as follows:

- I will *conclude* what I am through the information I am supplied by the environment I am placed in and accept as true.

- I will know who and what I am by the *behavioral outcomes and linguistic information* I receive and experience.
- I will know who and what I am by my success at fulfilling my needs and wants or lack thereof.
- I will know who and what I am by the physical treatment I receive from my caregivers and others who are in my immediate environment.
- I will know who and what I am by my accumulation of the data I am given about myself coupled with the outcome (environmental responses) of those things I do to test my hypotheses about who I am and what I am capable of doing.
- My conclusions will establish my "existential life position" in the "OK Corral. (Existential life positions will be discussed in the section on transactional analysis. The notion of "life positions" was first proposed by Dr. Franklin Ernst, Jr. in 1964.[59]

Sir Frederick Bartlett is credited with the notion of schemas, which he developed while he was studying how memory works and why it fails when it does.[60]

Jean Piaget was participating in the study of intelligence when he began the rigorous observation of how children learn to think. He has demonstrated the developmental stages of thinking, how it moves from precausal thinking (ages two through seven) to concrete operations (ages seven through twelve) and finally to formal operations (ages eleven through fifteen or twenty). It is this developmental era between birth and seven years of age that is critical to our understanding of how early maladaptive schemas can be solidified in adolescents and impair formal operational thinking. Early maladaptive schemas lie at the heart of most severe addictive disorders. For a brief overview of the beliefs that are generated during these critical developmental stages, see this article on Wikipedia.[61]

Piaget's work was a possible intellectual precursor for, and added to our understanding of, the *personal constructs* that George Kelly later proposed. He became one of the pioneers of the recent cognitive behavioral movement with the publication of *The Psychology of Personal Constructs*.[62] Like Piaget, Kelly proposed that we are all scientists; we all have hypotheses about how the world works. Survival depends on the accuracy of these constructs. He proposed that we test our hypotheses so that we may refine them to improve their accuracy. As small children, we learn that a frown or a whimper will prompt a response from our caregivers because it communicates that we need something; as we mature, we must refine our model because they now expect a *please* and a *thank you* for their assistance.

Part of our conception of self is defined by *self-referents*, saying, "I am—" (For instance, insert *smart/dumb, attractive/unattractive, addicted/normal*, or *depressed/ happy*.) When you define yourself in certain ways, you must then conform to those definitions because failure to do so will create cognitive dissonance, a state of discomfort caused by your behaving in ways that are inconsistent with your constructs about who you think you are. The collections of constructs you have about anything and everything create your schemas.

Thanks in part to B. F. Skinner,[63] the rise of behaviorism in the 1950s, with the method's successful demonstration of the power of reinforcement in controlling behavior, relegated cognitive processes (which were unobservable and therefore not worth studying) to the back pages of academia. A resurrection of the contribution of cognition came twenty years later when new science created a *paradigm shift*. In 1967, Aaron Beck[64] began publishing his work on schemas and their relationship to psychological problems. Cognition and behaviorism amount to cognitive behaviorism.*

Linguistic Relativity

Our Idiosyncratic Perception Is Reality

Language is the symbolic representation of what's actually stored in the cognitive portion of the mind that determines our perception of the world. Once again, it is the uniqueness of our perception of reality that allows cognitive theorists to assert that the way we define ourselves is owing to our own peculiar worldview. The relativity part asserts that we understand that even though we use the same words to describe things, it does not imply that the events we are describing are, in fact, the same. When an adult seeks treatment for a substance-use disorder, we conduct a biopsychosocial assessment during which we ask about his or her childhood. The response *it was normal* can mean a great many different things; it will not mean the same for a person who grew up in a crime family as it will for a person who grew up in a devoutly religious household. It is critical to our search for antecedent causes that we acknowledge that those persons' views of the world and their places in it are vastly different. Curiously, either household can be contributory to developing early maladaptive schemas.

Katherine Nelson presents the position in the following way:

---

* Overviews of Skinner and Beck are on Wikipedia; see endnotes.

Although language is central to the story worked out here it rests on prior non-linguistic perceptual, conceptual, and social-communicative processes. Thus it is not separable from cognitive development generally, and the reverse is also true: cognitive development is not separable from language. To understand these relations, it is important, in my view, to take an experiential view of development in which individual development over time is the focus. The theoretical approach developed in this book is an *experiential* one. In this perspective, the child as an acting and interacting person is always in view. What the child represents of the world she experiences is a function of the purposes enshrined in her current concerns, which change over time. The resulting representations constitute the filtered products of a developmental history, in turn providing the context within which new experiences are interpreted and represented. One of the central claims of this approach is that *the primary cognitive task of the human child is to make sense of his or her situational place in the world in order to take a skillful part in its activities.* This is an imperative for the human child—unlike virtually all nonhuman animals—because of the highly variable conditions that may be met in human societies, beyond some very basic similarities.[65]

She also presents the following basic question: "How does an individual child begin to acquire knowledge of the specific circumstances of her life and world and to adapt to those circumstances effectively in order to take part within its social and cultural activities?"

This is an adequate description of what *survival strategies* are. We define ourselves by what we do, how we behave, and—in some instances—even the fact that we have impure thoughts, at least according to certain belief systems (the thought is as bad as the deed). The linguistic systems we define ourselves with determine our worth. My experience with substance abusers, especially long-term abusers, is that they hold themselves in extremely low esteem and even contempt; they consider themselves to be "lower than whale shit," or something that is lower than what is on the bottom of the ocean. They have no idea that their *perception* of their early environments warped their ability to be normal.

The terms they use to refer to themselves are deplorable: terms like *crack whore, slut, pimp, thief, abuser,* and *bad parent* They use these self-destructive words because serious addiction typically requires the violation of social mores. When they present for treatment, it is imperative to help them differentiate between *who they are* and *what they have done.* That is, we need to separate the *behavior* from the *person.* This does not imply that the behavior is condoned but that it is understood in the context of those behavioral adaptations associated with substance-use disorder and avoiding withdrawal during active addiction. By perceived necessity, they'll say things like, "I'm dope sick" or "I have the shakes," thus allowing the decision maker of the personality to reside with an immature, perhaps even infantile version of the personality and its associated schemas. Research on the *models of decision making* reliably demonstrates that short-term gratification takes precedence over postponement of gratification, even if postponing gratification would bring a bigger reward.

I smoked cigarettes until I was fifty-six years old. I quit when I finally acknowledged that cigarettes were harmful to my health—when I put an end to my denial. I do not introduce myself by saying, "Hello. I'm Dr. Wilson, and I'm a smoker," yet milligram per milligram, nicotine is as addictive as heroin. In fact, the Center for Disease Control (CDC) notes that nicotine is responsible for approximately 480,000 deaths per annum. The reality is that I no longer smoke and do not plan to take it up ever again. I refuse to define myself by a behavior I have given up; it is not part of who I am, despite the fact that it is a part of who I was.

This anecdote is in service of addressing some aspects of AA treatment that may be a violation of sound therapeutic intervention and self-affirmation. I understand your fear that, if you do not identify yourself as an addict and/or alcoholic, you may become complacent grandiose regarding your ability to manage your drug of choice and assume that the neural pathway you've been down thousands of times no longer exists. Although you haven't been using it lately, it is still there; it's not as strong as it was during your active addiction, but it is lying in wait, ready to be reactivated. It is critical to recognize the power of the words we use to define ourselves and how they affect our behavior. "I am what I think I am!"

Hardware and Software: *Tabula Rasa*

Hardware is built in to the brain; it already knows what its functions and purposes are. *Software* is the conscious part of the mind. The brain operates primarily below conscious awareness.

In 1689, John Locke[66] expanded on Greek Stoicism by proposing that we are all born with a blank slate, otherwise known as a *tabula rasa*. He was addressing the issue of the contents of the conscious *mind* and proposed that humans are born with the *potential to acquire information by being exposed to it*—that the contents of the mind (the software) are acquired through perception and experience. Thus, whatever your experiences are—whatever conclusions you draw about how you will be treated, what you will become, and what you are—will be determined by the input and, more importantly, your *perception* of that input. If both parents wanted to provide more for their child by working, it is possible for that child to interpret their absence as abandonment. In another family, if both parents are alcoholics who are similarly unavailable, their child might also assume, "I have been abandoned." It is important to understand that *it is not the actual event but one's interpretation of the event that dictates how the schema will develop.* In the eyes of a two-year-old, you are either there or not there. "We are simply trying to provide for you" will fall on deaf ears, because the two-year-old doesn't understand what *provide* means.

Early Schemas Are, in Fact, Survival Strategies

It is imperative that very young children acquire the techniques and develop the strategies that will allow their basic survival needs to be met. They have no mobility and depend entirely on the cooperation of the older people around them, who must feed them, clothe them, and meet their other basic survival needs. The strategies that we develop become the schemas we live by. They become our *survival strategies.* Human beings are born with probably the least amount of hardwired behavior, even though we have an extremely complex nervous system that operates beneath the surface to regulate our biological processes. In reality, it takes close to two decades to bring a newborn up to speed so that he or she can become a successful adult. The information we absorb during this two-decade-long process influences our survival strategies. Imagine that you grew up in a crime family in which antisocial behavior is not only the norm but also reinforced by scapegoating the "square johns," "ham-and-eggers," and "nine-to-fivers" who are too dumb to understand that you can earn more in an hour of selling drugs than they can in a month of working a forty-hour-a-week job. *Honesty is the best policy* is probably not part of this family's survival strategy.

Competence, Motivation, and Survival Strategies

Survival requires having a moderately accurate set of facts about the world around us and the ability to operate within that environment successfully. What that means is that we need sufficiently accurate information on how we can get our needs and wants met, at least on a subsistence level. Competence, then, is our ability to get what we need and want in our own unique way. Needs are differentiated from wants; they are what we actually need to survive, such as air, food, water, elimination, and sleep. If we are deprived of any one of these things for a sufficient amount of time, we will expire. Once we successfully meet any of our needs or wants, we start to build a repertoire of schemas about how we can do just that. When we find a strategy that produces one of our desired results, we begin to solidify our facts about the world and figure out how to make our way in it.

One of the goals we all want to achieve is the ability to get what we need and want with the minimum amount of effort on our part. When we establish a relationship between a particular behavior or set of behaviors that meets a need or a want, we reach a state of equilibrium, which is the objective of our basic biology. We will practice that sequence until it is well inculcated in our repertoire. When the need or want is unfulfilled, this causes stress and creates a state of disequilibrium. Stress tells the mind or brain that some issue needs resolution, and until the stress is reduced, it will remain an irritant. Physical or psychological stress activates the fight-or-flight syndrome; this activation releases adrenaline, and only fighting or fleeing will dissipate it. Unfortunately, in today's world, fighting and fleeing are both frowned upon. The inability or refusal to fight or flee causes the adrenaline to break down into serum cortisol, which creates agitation. Once this happens, it's difficult to concentrate, relax, or sleep. Exercise and meditation are two ways to remove the serum cortisol from your system.

Some survival strategies are actually preconscious, or below conscious verbal awareness, as we did not have a sufficient vocabulary or the conceptual skills to describe them when we first developed them. Children begin verbalizing between two and three years of age. Therefore, it is doubtful that the vocabulary of a one-year-old could construct the following internal dialogue: *If I scream loudly enough and long enough, somebody will come to change my diaper and feed me. In fact, there is a neural pathway being built between meeting the biological need (hunger) and what I think I did to reduce the biological stress caused by my being hungry.* Of course, neural pathways are being built by an association between what the developing infant does that produces the appropriate environmental response that reduces biological tension.. There's an association built up in the developing mind that attaches crying, smiling, or other such behaviors to getting one's needs met. This matter has been addressed by the burgeoning field of *neural plasticity*, or the study of *how the brain forms and maintains synaptic connections.* These very early synaptic connections between our actions and their effects on the environment become the basis for our schemas about our life and overall survival. Suffering trauma at this stage is the precursor to developing early maladaptive schemas. Why are my needs not being met? How will I meet them? Who will help me? What conclusions am I drawing about my place in the world?

Software (schemas) consists of the mental structures that we humans can use to communicate with others and perform operations like typing this manuscript, solving math problems, going online to find information, and so on. Software is essentially an add-on that is created by experience and established by the principles of learning. The software we keep is software we find useful—that is, whatever *produces the personally rewarding outcomes we expect.* We sort the information we receive on how the world works into what are called *schemas* or *scripts.* Our survival is dependent upon the accuracy of our software, and that software is every bit as important as the brain cells that operate it. We call our software *core beliefs*, *cognitive structures*, and *worldviews* because it determines how we view the world and our position in it. Our very survival is dependent upon our ability to predict outcomes and adapt to their demands.

Consider this inclusive definition of *schemas* from a psychological point of view:

> In psychology and cognitive science, a schema (plural schemata or schemas) describes a pattern of thought or behavior that organizes categories of information and the relationships among them. It can also be described as a mental structure of preconceived ideas, a framework representing some aspect of the world, or a system of organizing and perceiving new information. Schemata influence attention and the absorption of new knowledge: people are more likely to notice things that fit into their schema, while reinterpreting contradictions to the schema as exceptions or distorting them to fit. Schemata have a tendency to remain unchanged, even in the face of contradictory information. Schemata can help in understanding the world and the rapidly changing environment. People can organize new perceptions into schemata quickly as most situations do not require complex thought when using schema, since automatic thought is all that is required. People use schemata to organize current knowledge and provide a framework for future understanding. Examples of schemata include academic rubrics, social schemas, stereotypes, social roles, scripts, worldviews, and archetypes. In Piaget's theory of development, children construct a series of schemata, based on the interactions they experience, to help them understand the world.[67]

What Is the Source of Your Addiction Schema?

As small children, we develop schemas about how *our* world is going to respond to the behaviors we engage in. Before we have the language necessary to express *our* needs and wants, we use emotion to communicate with the unique world we live in—*our world*, not the world in general. When we are very young, we do not have the core beliefs, cognitive structures, or logic systems we need to refute inaccurate input from our immediate environment—input that is maladaptive to healthy development. Information about who we are, what we are, and what we're going to be is being indelibly written on our *tabula rasa*. If left unrefuted, this early information will play a major role in *how we treat ourselves*, especially if the information is negative. Schemas we develop that allow us to be treated in unhealthy ways, whether by others or by ourselves, are called *early maladaptive schemas* (EMSs). I will discuss these in detail in the section on early maladaptive schemas and transactional analysis.

One of the major problems in our current treatment of addiction is that we pay too little attention to software and too much attention to hardware. Therefore, one of the critical tools that will aid in our understanding of addiction is knowing how the brain and mind interact with each other to control our actions. It is important that we acknowledge software's role in this interaction and perhaps even give it preeminent status in our attempts to understand addiction.

It is not generally understood that the interaction between the mind and the brain goes both ways. When we are able to see how brain processes are proceeding, we can learn to affect them through biofeedback. It is possible to observe brainwaves, heartbeat, respiration, blood pressure, and various other biological activities through monitoring devices. Once we can observe such things, we can also alter them simply by thinking about them. Exercise, meditation, and mindfulness, for instance, actually alter biological activity. The ability of the mind to alter biological processes such as physiological cravings is critical to treating addiction.

Pragmatic Absolute: Survival Is the Brain's Primary Job

Some organisms that are lower on the phylogenetic scale (having smaller, less complicated brains with less cerebral cortex) are born "hardwired." Snakes are abandoned by their mother at the laying of the eggs they are born in; when they hatch, they are fully equipped to survive without any parental training. The newborn snake already knows what to do when something in its heat-sensing field is warm and will fit in its mouth: bite it, wait for it to weaken, and then swallow it headfirst. The hardware is built in and requires little or no experience to operate. I have even seen patients who had been lobotomized and were therefore devoid of emotion but still alive and functioning.

How Does the Brain Execute the First Pragmatic Absolute?

The brain monitors all of the systems of the body without any conscious input from us. It does this by having genetically preset values that any particular system *should* operate at. For instance, most body temperatures are preset at 98.6° Fahrenheit. My normal body temperature is 97.6°, so I must inform medical personnel that my temperature is worthy of note at 100.6°, not the standard 101.6°. There are also sensors in your carotid arteries (in your neck) that measure the amount of oxygen in your bloodstream. We have all inherited slight differences in our familial genetic presets. One of the findings in our studies of alcoholism is that some people have large amounts of alcohol dehydrogenase, so they can process more alcohol per given time than those who have less. This difference in one's ability to process large amounts of alcohol without becoming intoxicated can lead one to believe that he or she is "immune" to becoming an alcoholic. Habitual use results in the same false information.

Equilibrium Is the Goal

Both the brain and the mind depend on feedback to determine whether systems are operating properly—that the tools used to create a steady state (equilibrium) are working at all. If I've exercised too stringently and raised my internal body temperature, I have to wonder if the process of sweating is actually reducing my body temperature. If my built-in unconscious processes do not produce the desired reduction in temperature, heatstroke becomes possible and I will need to turn to external strategies (ice baths). On the other hand, if it's cold outside and I'm not properly dressed, does the shaking and shivering (muscle contractions) raise my body temperature? One of the many tools the brain uses to monitor our automatic functions is homeostasis, which—loosely translated from the Greek—means *remains the same*. In the previous scenarios, would whatever corrective measure I chose to employ return my adaptive system to a steady state? Some addicts mix cocaine (a stimulant) and heroin (a depressant) in the same syringe to obtain such a state while some alcoholics mix uppers (stimulants) with alcohol to vitiate the central nervous system's depressed effects of alcohol.

Remember, like the previously described snake, we too possess some "hardwiring." We have functions that are *hardwired*, such as maintenance functions that operate without any input from our mind (*software*). We are unaware of the process of glandular secretions, such as the secretion of insulin to regulate blood-sugar levels, and the continuous production of red blood cells from the marrow in our long bones.

Nevertheless, without these automatic functions, we would not survive. It is also important to understand that the brain's job is to maintain homeostasis, a state where there is neither positive nor negative deviation from a set internal biological standard. Why is this important? Deviations from a neutral state cause stress, and stress alerts us that something isn't as it should be. Both the brain and mind must find ways to reduce these undesirable states.

The brain has sensors for all of those automatic processes so that it knows when there is a deviation from the set standard. When there is such a deviation, the brain activates corrective mechanisms. Most body temperatures are around 98.6° Fahrenheit. When the body drops below that temperature, the brain institutes corrective mechanisms like shaking and shivering (rapid muscle contractions), to produce heat, and piloerection, which traps heat around the body. When we work hard, the activity of our muscles generates heat, and this raises the body's temperature. The brain knows that it is not good when our temperature deviates from the preset value (fevers can kill brain cells), so it activates temperature-reduction techniques like perspiration. This same process occurs for conditions we are unaware of or do not even think about. When we have too much sugar in our blood, the brain (*hardware*) notifies the pancreas to secrete insulin, a process that the mind (*software*) actually has no conscious awareness of as it occurs on a chemical/cellular level.

Hardware and Software Cooperate for Our Survival

When we examine another *feedback loop*, we are able to observe *a software and hardware interaction*. The fight-or-flight response, for example, is activated when we *perceive a biological or psychological threat*. As one of our *hardwired survival strategies*, when we perceive a threat (*software*), our body prepares to fight or flee—whichever is most likely to ensure our survival. It accomplishes this feat by activating the adrenal glands, which then flood the system with adrenaline. The introduction of adrenaline increases our visual and auditory acuity, redistributes our blood to large muscles and away from digestive processes, narrows the blood vessels in our face (areas where we bleed profusely), stiffens our hairs to conserve heat (piloerection), and initiates a host of other physiological processes associated with survival. It makes no difference whether you attribute this response to evolution or intelligent design; the activation process exists to ensure our survival. This mechanism was particularly useful in times when the fight-or-flight response was more prevalent. Indeed, there was a time in our history when fleeing and fighting were our only two options for dealing with threats. Now, we hire a lawyer and litigate, or we buy guns and shoot people. Using the Marquis of Queensbury rules is no longer a viable option for settling disputes. It is interesting that we outlawed dueling and now, with the proliferation of guns, seem to be taking a step backward.

Here is a concrete example of how a long held schema can be altered by new facts. Many of my friends and acquaintances have opted to obtain permits to carry concealed weapons. I did not perceive the need to do so. However, as I write this (May 9, 2015), the media are telling me that my safety has been severely compromised by direct threats from ISIS. The militant ISIS group has issued a threat targeting any and all Americans, and that includes me and mine. I now perceive a very real—not imagined—threat to my life. My first thought is whether I should go get my carry permit for a concealed weapon so that I can protect my family and myself. My self-preservation *schema* now tells me that there are people out in the world who believe it is OK to kill my family members, friends, and acquaintances simply because we're not Muslim—and they won't forewarn me of that belief. I now feel the need to be hypervigilant of others in my environment, and I will be profiling. Dressing as a Goth (in dark or black attire) could have serious consequences on your health. Why? Black is the stereotypical attire of ISIS/ISSL extremists. My schema for extremists has been created primarily by the media presentations of the unprovoked attacks on Muslims and non-Muslims alike: Muslims who do not share their fundamental beliefs, Muslims of a different sect, and non-Muslim Westerners.

Today (June 13, 2016), I am proofreading and adding new information to my manuscript a day after the atrocity in Orlando, where an obviously disturbed individual murdered forty-nine people and injured fifty-three others at a gay nightclub. I would be saddened by this kind of unprovoked attack on any community, let alone the LGBTQ community, who have long suffered because of the prevailing schemas about sexuality. My need for hypervigilance is not affected as I neither fit the description of those who were attacked nor frequent nightclubs, and there have been few demonstrable attacks in the environs that I inhabit.

There is an undesired side effect to this particular process; more often than not, we are not allowed to fight or flee due to social prohibitions against both violence and cowardice. The inability to physically burn off the energy generated by the adrenal activation leaves us with a byproduct of the breakdown of adrenaline (serum cortisol), which is very discomforting as it produces severe agitation. In behavioral terms, this is a punishment. All perceived threats to our self-esteem, character, and control over or access to secondary reinforcers (like our job) activate the flood of adrenaline. As addicts, you know how to deal with anxiety and can thus calm the adrenal beast.

Consider persons who deal with snakes on an everyday basis. Herpetologists do not experience the flight-or-fight reaction that many of us do when faced with a snake. Their software allows them to know which snakes are overly dangerous/venomous, which cues indicate that a snake is about to become aggressive, and so on. As a result, they do not identify the snakes they deal with as a threat to their survival, and so, their adrenal glands are not activated.

Fear is a learned physiological response to particular stimuli that have no ability to evoke a response of any kind until we assign that power to them through our *software*. Children are not born afraid of snakes, spiders, or skulls and crossbones on containers; they need to be trained to assign either a positive or negative value to those cues.

We are all unique. None of us have the exact same set of built-in biological standards that come with the shared genetic complement given to us by our parents. Even monozygotic (paternal) twins, who have almost identical *hardware*, do not share the same *software*.

CHAPTER 3

New Science: Early Environments, ACEs, and Trauma

The Role of Trauma in Addiction

There is a whole separate body of literature related to the physical, psychological, behavioral, and societal consequences of adverse childhood experiences that deserves discussion. They are the Adverse Childhood Experience (ACE) Study, Longitudinal Studies of Child Abuse and Neglect (LONGSCAN), and the National Survey of Child and Adolescent Well-Being (NSCAW).[68] From each I will draw reported data that bears on the relationship between ACEs, early maladaptive schemas (EMSs), and the subsequent self-destructive behavior. What I don't find in the literature is any empirical assessment of one's perceived lovability. My clinical experience suggests that this is a significant, perhaps even critical, variable, lovability, in ones ability to insulate oneself from self-destructive behavior. Is this one of the resilience factors? (Dissertation topic anyone?)

With seventeen thousand participants, the ACE Study is a significant one—and it is difficult to quibble with its empirical relevance when it has that sample size. Its findings support everything that's been presented so far with respect to dysfunctional childhood environments and the subsequent self-destructive behavior. The basic factors affecting the consequences of child abuse and neglect are

- the child's age and developmental status at the time of occurrence;
- the type of abuse, neglect, or other maltreatment (physical, sexual, and/or psychological);
- the frequency, duration, and severity of the maltreatment; and

- the relationship between the child and the abuser. The ACE study motivated extensive research of the effects of ACEs on normal development. The following research validates a significant maladaptive relationship across a variety of cognitive and behavioral dimensions:

  - One study using ACE Study data found that roughly 54 percent of cases of depression in women and 58 percent of suicide attempts in women were connected to ACEs.[69]

  - According to Messmen-Morre et al., dysregulation is impacted by childhood mistreatment, which often persists into adolescence and adulthood.[70]

  - NSCAW reported severe developmental and cognitive difficulties; 43 percent had emotional or behavioral trauma, and 13 percent of the sample had both. More than half of the youth who present for maltreatment are at risk of developing an emotional problem, grade repetition, substance abuse, delinquency, truancy, or pregnancy.[71]

  - Child sexual abuse results in an increase in sexual risk-taking, and in adolescence, it can raise the risk of contracting a sexually transmitted disease (STD). There is a strong relationship between child sexual abuse and the risk of rape in adulthood.

  - Parental neglect is associated with borderline personality disorders, attachment issues, or affectionate behaviors with unknown or little-known people, inappropriate modeling of adult behavior, and aggression.[72]

  - Children who have experienced abuse are *nine times more likely to become involved in criminal activities*[73]

Alcohol and other drug abuse plays a role. V. J. Felitti reports that "research consistently reflects an increased likelihood that children who have experienced abuse or neglect will smoke cigarettes, abuse alcohol, or take illicit drugs during their lifetime. In fact, male children with an *ACE score of 6 or more (having 6 or more adverse childhood experiences) had an increased likelihood—of more than 4,600 percent—to use intravenous drugs later in life.*"

Obtain your ACE score on page 160 Additional info available online @ ACES Score

Maladaptive Schemas Are the Result of Trauma, Real or Perceived

> *Your secrets keep you sick!*
> —AA/NA SLOGAN

When all of the explanations are stripped away, addictions are ultimately *self-destructive behaviors* and *self-fulfilling prophecies*. These are behaviors that result in negative physical, legal, medical, financial, psychological, moral, and social consequences in the broadest and most inclusive sense: rejection, alienation, ostracism, isolation, and/or legal consequences. Trauma can be real or perceived. It is important to remember that one need not be the direct object of the trauma. To witness self-destructive behavior or be a participant in it in any way is sufficient to cause you trauma. When our daughter lost her battle with triple-negative breast cancer, my wife and I were with her for the entire two-year ordeal. Thinking about what she might have been thinking about—her fears and her pains—was *and is* traumatic for us. Not all of the servicemen and -women involved in defending our country, on both foreign and domestic soil, suffer from PTSD. Why not? There are several psychological processes that buffer us from trauma. Some of the psychological techniques we develop include isolation, intellectualization, rationalization, suppression, and repression. It is our ability to accurately insulate ourselves from what we observe and are not directly a part of that protects us from being traumatized by an event. When we come up with an acceptable explanation, that excludes *us as the object* of the traumatic event, it is not traumatic to us. When we do not or cannot define the traumatic event as not pertinent to our life, we suffer trauma; we end up with disorders like survivors' guilt, secondary trauma, vicarious trauma, or PTSD. Primary responders, mental-health professionals, and those of us who are simply privy to the traumas of those we treat can produce secondary trauma.

Where do early maladaptive schemas emanate from? How are they created? Children do not have the psychological coping mechanisms necessary to rationalize the behavior of the adults around them. They have not developed the necessary concepts and verbal skills to make sense of the behavior of those around them. They know only that they're *hungry, uncomfortable, frightened, in physical pain, alone, physically accosted, and so on.* Thus, they develop a maladaptive schema about how safe the environment is. What is stored in the memory banks of a one-year-old who has been crying because of a diaper rash and is spanked for continuing to cry? The infant is incapable of constructing a sentence stating, "My needs are not being met because those responsible for my care are incapable of or not interested in providing it."

Since it is a requirement of survival that we make sense of our environment, the fact that our caregivers are not attending to our needs must imply that there is something about us that makes us unworthy of care. And so develops a maladaptive schema regarding getting our needs met. If we are the victim of physical or sexual abuse (once again lacking the ability to rationalize the behavior of the perpetrators), we wrongly assume that we somehow deserve that behavior or that some negative quality of ours prompted them to violate us. Maladaptive schemas can be acquired any time during our lifespan. It is important to understand that they can come from the way we are treated at school, church, or the local playground, on the Internet, or any other place where you can and probably will be evaluated by your peers.

If you lack sufficient ego strength—the resilience to defend yourself from cruel invective—you will suffer a decrease in your worth. We are painfully aware of the cruelty children can inflict upon their peers who do not fit in because they are different in any way. The list of characteristics that result in exclusion by one's peers is almost limitless. You need do nothing more than transfer into a school where most friendships and cliques have already been established. Your social status, ethnicity, hair color, clothing, grades, whether you're good at sports, and any deviation from the existing group norms can leave you isolated. Most kids from divorced families find other kids in the same situation to hang out with. Most of the isolated kids will tell you that the stoners (substance users and abusers) are accepting of all who *feel or believe they are socially rejected*. The price of admission to the stoners' club is the willingness to participate in substance use—inhale, inject, or ingest, and you earn instant acceptance! The corollary benefit of joining the substance users is the elimination of the *parent ego state*, which is the conscience, or the rule giver who commands, "Don't do that." Nicotine, alcohol, and other mood elevators allow some relief from self-destructive thoughts and this sort of internal dialogue and can also produce in most a feeling of worth. When I ask the addiction population what was positively reinforcing about consuming mood-altering substances, they answer, "I felt good enough about myself that I could talk to members of the opposite sex and felt that I fit in with a group." Communication becomes easier among their peers because the parental command to not look foolish is eliminated as well. You will find a complete discussion of the ego states in the section on subpersonalities.

In my considered opinion, it is imperative to your recovery that you understand that many of our addictive behaviors *have their roots in early software issues* and our conditioned responses *to real or perceived threats* to our psychological and physiological integrity. Remember, *my perception is my reality*. Schemas and scripts are just like hardware. When some issue in the environment is *inconsistent* with your schema, you attempt to alter it. Because it causes stress, you want to return to homeostasis. For example, let's assume someone finds you attractive and attempts to give you a compliment. Your schema doesn't allow you to believe that you are attractive, so you must find a way to alter the reality of the compliment. You might make it consistent with your maladaptive schema by thinking that the person only wants something from you, is making fun of you, or is just being polite. The point is that the maladaptive schema remains in place, but you don't get to feel better about yourself, and so, a positive reinforcement is lost. Strike another blow to your self-esteem! You just surrendered to your maladaptive schema.

What Does All of This Have to Do with Addiction?

- There are hardware activities that are constantly in operation beneath our software's radar. Some of them are responses to conditioned stimuli that were previously neutral (i.e., cues). For instance, bottles of a certain shape, crystals of a certain shape and color, paraphernalia that is typically paired with mind-altering substances, pills of certain shapes and colors, and certain types of cigarette lighters have been linked to self-medication and taken on the ability to elicit drug-seeking properties. As defined here, psychotropics are substances not produced by the brain that can act like substances that *are* produced by the brain (neurotransmitters). The brain operates by exchanging information among its cells.

- The process of activating communication among brain cells is called *neural transmission*. Some of these conditioned responses are what we refer to as the *triggers* that can (*but not must*) precede and initiate relapse behaviors. If you understand that the urge doesn't represent a moral failing or lack of willpower on your part, and that it is simply your hardware's response to things you have *repeatedly paired far too many times in the past,* it is not necessary for you to succumb to it. The average craving lasts only between five and seven minutes. I know you *can* be patient, but *are you willing to be?* Both AA and NA challenge members to "do the next right thing" for five to seven minutes.

- Cellular disruptions that occur in our brain disrupt our "hardwired" functions when they introduce substances that the brain did not produce and that can cross the blood-brain barrier. This blood-brain barrier was designed to keep most chemicals out of the delicate and well-modulated biochemical/electrical system that makes the autonomic, sympathetic, and parasympathetic nervous systems work. Its balance is delicate, so when we accidentally believe we can fly and attempt to do so, it is because we have upset the biochemical system. We will discuss how psychoactive substances alter the automatic operations of the brain in the section on psychopharmacology. This will explain why we stop eating, sleeping, or supplying self-care; alter our perceptions; and shift from occasional recreational substance use to addiction.

- It is time to focus more on the psychological software *maladaptive schemas* and the *traumas that produce them and allow us to initiate behaviors that are self-destructive.* It is time to understand that your belief in your inability to stop hurting yourself is inaccurate. Abstinence is possible, but many of the beliefs you hold about yourself are what drive you to persist in self-destructive behavior. Luckily, these self-defeating beliefs are both discoverable and treatable.

- It is important to remember that the interaction between the hardware and the software goes both ways. The hardware can introduce feelings, and those feelings can in turn alter the hardware. The notion of biofeedback is the effect the mind has on the actions of the brain. If you scrutinize the facial expression of a depressed patient telling a joke, you will notice that it changes into a smile and that the tone of the patient's voice also becomes markedly different.

Remember, we have approximately 86 billion nerve cells in our brain; 16.9 billion (about 18 percent) of them are located in the cerebral cortex, where most of the *conscious* activity occurs.

A critical corollary related to the cerebral cortex is that it is not fully developed until we are in our twenties. Dr. Frances Jensen,[75] discusses the relationship between the incomplete development of this mind portion of the brain and how it is the seat of executive decision making. During adolescence, this executive decision making includes the postponement of gratification, appropriate social behavior, impulse control, moral development, and long-term planning. Much of a chronic abuser's addictive behavior begins in adolescence, while their frontal cortex is still developing. So many of the strategies developed during this period are not put into practice. This results in inaccurate reality testing of the consequences of substance abuse and dependence.

The next section offers a fairly detailed description of how the mind and the brain acquire and maintain useful information. It helps to understand the *idiosyncratic* nature of the behavior that is accepted into, and that which is rejected from, our behavioral repertoire. The reward centers of the brain are instrumental in what we learn, but no learning happens without input from *the mind*. The section on maladaptive sche-mas and subpersonalities (or transactional analysis) follows in Chapter 5 and Chapter 4 may be a bit tedious, but the information is critical to understanding why maladaptive behavior is emitted.

CHAPTER 4

New Science: Creating a Paradigm Shift in Learning

What Are the Principles Governing Behavior Acquisition?

There is an entire city in Nevada that exists because the *principles of reinforcement* work extremely well. That city is Las Vegas. The casinos compete by proudly boasting they have a 97 percent payout rate on their slot machines. How can they survive on a 3 percent return and give good food at a discount, drinks at the tables, and operate slot machines? They know that a *variable ratio,* a *variable interval schedule of reinforcement,* will keep you pouring your money into the slot until it is all gone! The payouts at random intervals and of random size convince you that there is a pot of gold at the end of the one-armed bandit's rainbow.

This section is specifically for addiction professionals and professional addicts. The purpose is to integrate learning theory into your understanding of *your addiction.* You can't treat it until you own it. It's not *an* addiction, or *the* addiction, it's *my* or *your* addiction. And who knows more about your addiction than you do? When we apply the well-established laws that govern the acquisition and maintenance of behaviors, much of the mystique surrounding addiction is eliminated. In this module, you will learn about

- the effect of classical conditioning on the *triggers that elicit negative behavior;*
- the role of operant conditioning in *maintaining behavior;*
- the role of modeling (observing and learning from others); and
- how behaviors are changed.

Understanding *how* a behavior is developed, maintained, and *extinguished* (eliminated) will allow *you* to eliminate *self-destructive behaviors* from *your repertoire.* When (or if) you have decided that the AA model is your road to sobriety, this knowledge will add to your understanding of the value of maintaining a relationship with the recovering community and having a sponsor, the role of accountability, and why concepts like 90 in 90 or mandates to do the next right thing are so important in establishing and maintaining sobriety following rehab. The principles of learning remain the same regardless of the treatment strategy you choose to employ.

In this section, the items in italics are terms and ideas that will aid in your understanding of your addiction. It would be useful to add them to your *repertoire* if they are not already there. Please consult the accompanying glossary for more information.

How Is Behavior Learned?

A Chronically Relapsing Brain Disease—or Simply a System Property?

The chronically relapsing brain-disease hypothesis posits that the brain has been permanently altered, structurally and functionally, by addiction—which is proved by the fact that relapse can occur even after long periods of sobriety. Corollary to that is that the genetic complement of the addict was, at the very least, contributory. So, one day, the addiction will magically reassert itself just because it can. In science, we call that a circular argument. A genetic predisposition caused the addiction that hijacked the brain, which permanently altered it. That is the rationale why a permanently altered brain can relapse at any time without reason.

The system-property argument has fewer steps and is far simpler. In science, we use Occam's razor, the principle that states we should accept the explanation with the fewest assumptions. What we know is that neural pathways are created and strengthened through practice. The more frequently the practice, the stronger the memory trace. Once you learn how to ride a bike, that information is stored in case you want to do it again. Similarly, once the memory trace for addictive behavior is established, it stays available, in case you need or want it at some time in the future. Nicotine is estimated to be at least as addictive as heroin on a milligram-for-milligram basis. How many cigarettes can you smoke in a day? How many days have you smoked? How strong is that neural pathway? You do the math.

Recall that approximately 20 percent of our brain cells are reserved for executive function—for the decision-making part of the brain that we can observe by listening to the "dialogue" that goes on during decision making. (This part of our brain consists primarily of the *prefrontal* and *frontal cortices*.) A consensus occurs only when the subpersonalities have each had their say, the pros and cons have been examined, the probabilities have been estimated, and the executive of the personality most likely to get the job done has been selected.

A behavioral sequence is established when brain cells form a pathway between a behavioral action and an outcome—*a reward that we want*. We have several reward centers in our brain, and they signal that any given mission has been accomplished. You think *I'm sated, not hungry or thirsty anymore* or *I feel loved and accepted*. That's how we know something has worked. Small children experiment with behaviors that produce responses from their environment. When they smile, we smile back or talk sweetly to, kiss, or cuddle them. A behavior is repeated when all the neurons in the brain have worked together to establish the necessary neural pathway. Every time that same behavior is duplicated and rewarded, that neural pathway is strengthened. When you do something many times, it becomes almost an automatic action. That is why relapse is so prevalent and seemingly so intransigent. When you have injected a psychoactive substance into your veins thousands of times, any cue related to that behavior can activate the relevant well-practiced neural pathway, leading to an accidental relapse. The schedules of reinforcement that follow will provide information on the power of reinforcement and the most successful ways to create behavioral sequences that are difficult to break. This information is another tool for your toolbox. Relapse is not a moral failing; it's the consequence of how we learn to survive.

Pragmatic Absolute: All Behavior Has a Purpose to the Organism Emitting It

Any discussion on learning requires an understanding of what happens to a living organism before and after it produces any given behavior. When you do anything in the presence of others, they will respond in one of four ways: with a positive reaction, a negative reaction, a neutral reaction, or no reaction at all (meaning that they will ignore you). Through this process, you establish a feedback loop with the outside world—not your internal concept of the world but your schema about the how the outside world works. The outcome of producing a behavior is called a *reinforcement* or *reward*.

Reinforcements are categorized in two basic ways. First, they have a valence, or a value: they can be positive (an R+), negative (an R-), neutral (an N) punishers (a P), or ignored. R+'s make us feel good and increase the likelihood that we will repeat a behavior. R-'s make us feel bad and are positively reinforcing when they are removed. Pretty simply, Ns have no effect on us, and Ps reduce the likelihood that we will repeat a behavior. Second, reinforcement can be either primary or secondary:

- *Primary reinforcers*, such as food, water, and psychotropics (drugs), have a direct effect on the body.
- *Secondary reinforcers* have a relationship with primary reinforcers. Money is a secondary reinforcer because—while you can use it to buy primary reinforcers—you can't eat it. (Well, I suppose you could, but I don't think it tastes very good!)

Cues Signal the Availability of Reinforcers.

Classical conditioning was first observed and described in the early 1900s by a Russian physiologist named Ivan Pavlov. Pavlov was studying the process of digestion and using dogs as his subjects. His intent was not to study conditioning, but—being an observant scientist—he noticed that when the lab assistants entered the room where the dogs were kept before the meat powder was dispensed, the dogs would begin to salivate. He observed that a neutral *stimulus* (the assistants) would not normally produce an unconditioned response (salivation) alone. But in this case, the mere sight of the people in white lab coats who had given meat powder to the dogs was capable of eliciting in them the response of salivation, even without the presentation of the meat powder. Pavlov continued to explore the connection between a stimulus and an unconditioned response by presenting a tone prior to the introduction of the meat powder. He was able to demonstrate that a tone alone was capable of eliciting the same *unconditioned physiological response* (salivation).

This was the beginning of our understanding of the relationship between events in the real world and our psychological and physiological responses to them. John B. Watson expanded on this concept in his famous (or perhaps infamous, by today's standards) Little Albert experiment, which consisted of conditioning the fear of a small, furry, white rabbit in an infant named Albert.[76] Watson was able to elicit fear in Little Albert by pairing the appearance of the rabbit with a loud (and thus scary) noise. Bad John.

Cues Are Triggers and Are Central to Our Understanding of Relapse in Addiction

Cues are both internal (interoceptive) and external (exteroceptive). Interoceptive cues signal a physical and/or psychological state—such as hunger, thirst, or a full bladder—and are of primary interest in the understanding of the relationship between addiction and *emotions*. We will treat emotions as cues when we discuss trauma, subpersonalities, early maladaptive schemas, and transactional analysis in the following chapters. *Emotions are critical to our understanding of addiction.*

Cues alert an individual to the availability of primary and secondary reinforcers; they represent learned relationships between a thing or event and its probable outcome. Some cues signal positive, rewarding outcomes (rewards) while others signal negative ones (punishments). A red light on the police car behind you is a cue that you could quite possibly face a negative consequence in the near future. The sight of a police car alone is a cue that it is time for you to pay strict attention to the speed limit, because you already know what the consequences are for failing to do so.

Triggers are not all bad. Advertising is all about triggers. The reason theaters show candy, sodas, and popcorn dripping with butter prior to a movie is to activate the connection in our mind/brain between those primary reinforcers and pleasure and ultimately direct us to the snack bar. Advertisers try to sell many products by suggesting that if we buy certain ones, we will obtain the favor of those we admire or desire—a very important primary reinforcement.

I have placed *triggers* in the category of classical conditioning because classical conditioning is how many cues are created. Further, one of the primary tenets of relapse prevention is *a change of persons, places, and things*. Why? Relapse is known to happen when a person is around the cues that were associated with his or her previous substance-use pattern. It is this automatic response to a cue that sets an operant chain in motion, and that terminates in that person using his or her drug of choice, that suggests the utility of cue exposure therapy (CET).[77] Some do argue, however, that it would be more effective if the syringe that is part of the exposure had actually been actually be inserted into the vein to complete the "draw" but no psychoactive substance available in its barrel.

Neural Plasticity

The behaviors we can see and evaluate all take place on a physiological substrate: the neuronal network of the mind. When we talk about the effects of rewards or punishments on behavior, we're talking about the reward systems of the brain. When we discuss the contribution to of the physiological substrate of addiction we are asking how we get to conscious awareness of the reward, the mind. It is beyond the scope of this book to discuss them in detail. However, it is important to understand that some of the reward centers are located where we process affective (emotional) responses.

When we attempt to look at any cues that motivate substance use and abuse, we typically talk about emotional (interoceptive) cues that serve as triggers for the desire to reduce stress that move us from equilibrium to disequilibrium. We can't see this particular neuronal pathway, but we can infer its existence. It is important to our understanding of the prevalence of relapse among the severely addicted. We learn when we can observe the relationship between a cue and its reward. The more we practice a particular behavior and receive our reward for doing so, the more automatic it becomes. More than fifty years ago, during my military service, I was required to respond with my serial number when responding to specific requests: "RA 19618710, sir." I don't even have to think about it now; I just know it. For only three of those years, it was important for me to know those letters and numbers to avoid a negative outcome. The consequence of responding incorrectly was quite costly.

Behaviors become automatic and appear on cue. When I think about a string of neurons that go "RA 19618710, sir," I am reminded that the neural "superhighway" is there. And so, the question becomes, how is repeated substance abuse any different when the disequilibrium of withdrawal, or the comfort of self-medication, has created such a neural superhighway in an addict's brain?

This is the *neural plasticity* piece of the addiction puzzle. When we repeat a behavior and obtain the same reward consistently over time, we create and strengthen a neural pathway. Because of this connection between conditioned stimuli and the response, the behavior demands less of our direct attention to both activate and complete. An external stimulus that has been regularly paired with substance abuse will trigger the behavior associated with substance abuse, and it will almost become automatic. This is how vigilance plays a part in recovery; it is possible to stop any given behavior by inserting a competing behavior into the behavioral sequence. Each time an old neural pathway is disrupted, a new one is strengthened. If you have repeated the negative behavior a thousand times, how many times must you replace it with a competing response before that competing response takes precedence?

This is true for both exteroceptive cues, such as beer ads, bottles, and "rigs" (injection paraphernalia), and interoceptive cues, such as feeling angry, sad, scared, glad, bored, stressed, frustrated, and so on. Threats to your ego, and the instability caused by co-occurring disorders like PTSD, depression, bipolar disorder, and anxiety, can follow.

A common disclaimer of rehabilitation is, "If you hang around the barbershop long enough, you are going to get a haircut!" What that means is that despite our best conscious intentions (willpower) of not responding to those persons, places, and things that are a part of our substance-abuse history, *our brain's response to them is automatic.* It takes an act of volition—a conscious decision of the *mind*—to recognize that an automatic response to a cue is about to be activated. When you have continually combined bottles, crack pipes, rolling papers, syringes, bars, the local crack house, your drug dealer's neighborhood, his or her car, and the people you drank or used other drugs with, even something as seemingly mundane as using your cell phone can trigger the process of classical conditioning. Classical conditioning then activates the conditioned response (substance use) because of the presence of the associated stimuli.

It is not a criticism of your resolve; this is simply how our brain operates to save time. Usually that is a good thing. If we had to actively process everything we did, we would experience "paralysis by analysis." Those of you who are IV drug users know that the rush begins with the decision to use, and then the baggy, the spoon, and the syringe come into play. Those of you who prefer alcohol know that your exposure to particular cues—passing by the bar or liquor store, seeing alcohol ads on TV, and even smoking (if you smoked while you drank)—are enough to trigger the desire to use. One of the hardest parts of my quitting nicotine was refraining from smoking as I was enjoying a beer or cocktail.

Operant Conditioning

Operant conditioning came into vogue in the 1950s with the work of B. F. Skinner. Whereas Pavlov studied the relationship of precedent events incapable of producing a physiological response (unconditioned stimuli) on behavior, Skinner studied the effects of the environmental consequences of behavior on the establishment and maintenance of behaviors. What Skinner discovered was that whether a behavior was positively reinforced (R+), negatively reinforced (R-), punished (P-), or ignored (N) would determine whether the behavior was likely to be repeated. What his experiments demonstrated was that there are multiple factors that control whether a behavior will be repeated or eliminated from one's repertoire and the strength with which it will be maintained. The salient factors included whether the *reward* was something the subject *wanted*, the *magnitude of the reward*, and the *schedules on which the reinforcements* (R+, R-, and P-) were *administered*. All of these factors affected the likelihood that the behavior would be repeated or eliminated from one's behavioral repertoire. One only need look at the behavior of those who gamble on one-armed bandits or lottery tickets to see the effects of the power of R+'s. Logic would tell us not to purchase a ticket for the lottery when the odds of winning are approximately 175,000,000:1, yet we do it anyway. Why? The magnitude of the reward—hundreds of millions of dollars—appeals to a part of our personality where magical thinking (the child subpersonality) rather than accurate reality testing (the adult subpersonality) gets to make the decision.

There are two factors that shed a tremendous amount of light on the relationship between the consequences of behavior; positive and negative reinforcers and the maintenance (repetition) of behaviors.

The first factor critical to our understanding of addictive behavior is the fact that *all behavior has a purpose*. What that means is that *all* behavior has a *meaningful purpose for us*. We may not always be consciously aware of what that purpose is, but there is always a purpose. The second factor is that *reinforcements are idiosyncratically defined*. This fact is critical to our understanding of why they exhibit what appear to be counterintuitive behaviors. The repetition of *self-destructive behavior* simply does not make any sense to us. The behavior appears to be counterintuitive because those observing the behavior—family, friends, therapists, law enforcement officers, the courts, and so on—would not purposely do anything to bring that outcome (*punishment, a P-*) *upon themselves*. What is not understood is that they get something that is positively rewarding for it (an R+). What you understand is that even though it appears to others that the consequences of your actions should be negative (e.g., derision, punishment, or rejection), to you, only rewards (e.g., the sensation of using your drug of choice) await. This is the only way this behavior makes any sense and helps to explain the maintenance (repeatability) of *self-destructive behaviors*. As an adolescent, I usually came to the negative attention of law enforcement when my stepfather was on duty and in uniform as a California highway patrolman. I received the full measure of his attention when he had to pick me up from the local PD in his CHP uniform.

Behavior is Idiosyncratically Defined

That *behavior is idiosyncratically defined* is a simple concept to illustrate. We all have preferences—for activities, entertainment, and food, for instance. Some among us work to buy vegetables like broccoli, kale, and Brussels sprouts while others avoid them like the plague. Some like tripe, collard greens, raw fish, sweetbreads, and pickled pig's feet, and stinky, mold-covered cheese. I know what is a rewarding reinforcement to you by what you are willing to work for (expend energy on, commit time to, and spend money on). For alcoholics, you do what is necessary to acquire alcohol; you stockpile it so you won't have to experience withdrawal. The same goes for nicotine. How many of you remember going through the ashtray looking for a butt to get a drag off in the morning? Your drug of choice is another indication of reinforcements being *idiosyncratically defined*. You have body-type preferences in who you choose to pursue for a relationship.

It is not much of an intellectual leap to acknowledge that our *self-destructive behaviors* are positively reinforcing to us (an R+) because we continue to emit them.

The first factor, *all behavior has purpose*, suggests that we are performing the behavior for some purpose that is *positively reinforcing to us*. Obviously, this relationship is clear when you are "dope sick" or experiencing the delirium tremens DTs from an alcohol overdose, because the most important thing to do is to remove the unpleasantness of the physical withdrawal that you are experiencing. By the time you've reached this stage of abuse, you know full well what it takes to relieve the physical discomfort of withdrawal, regardless of your drug of choice. There is nothing unclear about engaging in a self-destructive behavior (continued substance abuse) that will eliminate an unpleasant physical state of withdrawal (P), because it is obviously *positively reinforcing*.

Fact: the removal of a P (like the discomfort of withdrawal is a R-) positively reinforces an R+. What we know about positive reinforcement is that it increases the likelihood that the behavior will be repeated.

My self-destructive behavior that I described previously was done without any conscious thought. What is not so clear to those outside of us is how substance use or abuse is positively reinforcing to us. If the laws of behaviorism apply, then by some *anomalous process* (something is not wired correctly in our brain), self-destructive behavior is positively reinforcing to us. Although I did not recognize it at the time, having my stepfather come to the police station at night, when he was on duty and in full uniform, secured his attention in the only way I knew of. So, in retrospect, what seemed to be self-destructive—the violation of social and legal norms—served the purpose of meeting a *psychological need* to be acknowledged by the only father figure I knew. Unfortunately, this need generalized to the school environment as well, as I received lots of negative attention from school authorities too.

What makes our behavior so difficult to understand, for amateurs and professionals alike, is the *counterintuitive* nature of our *self-destructive* behavior. Having stuck our hand on the hot stove once, it will become obvious to others that we are crazy if we keep sticking our hand on the hot stove. "Why do you continue to do that to yourself?" they will ask. What they do not understand about us is that *the satisfaction of the psychological need is more powerful than the negative behavioral, social, and physiological consequences of our behavior*. I actually learned about the *idiosyncratic nature of reinforcement* in the '60s, but I did not understand its application to our *self-destructive* behavior until much later.

The Oxford Dictionary defines the *idiosyncratic nature of reinforcement* as "a peculiarity of constitution or temperament: an individualizing characteristic or quality," which means that you get to decide what is an R+ or R- or P for you.

One of the classes I was required to take as an undergraduate was a 300-level course entitled The Scientific Study of Behavior Modification. One of the course requirements was that you had to select a rat from the lab. In order to pass the course, you had to teach that rat a series of ten consecutive behaviors: ring a bell, climb a ladder, go through a tube, and so on. After two weeks of diligently attempting to teach my rat the sequence, I knew I had a developmentally delayed rat. I went to the professor, Dr. Morrow, and complained that I had inadvertently selected a developmentally delayed rat for my subject. I told him my rat was unable to learn the series of tasks as required. Dr. Morrow told me to return to the classroom and replay the film by Dr. Skinner. I dutifully rewound the film. Within the first five minutes, I knew what message Dr. Morrow had wanted me to hear: Dr. Skinner clearly stated that there was no such thing as a dumb subject, only a dumb experimenter! I returned to the professor's office, humbled.

"What am I missing?" I asked.

His response was simple: "What are you using for reinforcement R+?"

I glibly replied, "Rat chow."

His retort was, "Try Cocoa Puffs."

Needless to say, my rat became brilliant and learned the entire sequence in less than a week.

The moral of this true story is that no one can decide what is reinforcing for another organism. This leads us full circle to the moral of the story of learning: an explanation of our *apparently anomalous* counterintuitive acts that I call *self-destructive behavior*. The behaviors that those who care about us find inexplicable are positively reinforcing (R+'s) to us, or we would stop doing them. What is not recognized about continued *self-destructive behavior* is that as long as the *psychological need* driving the behavior remains unmet, we will continue to use a method that both soothes us (*self-medication*) and brings about some desired behavior from those around us. The unmet *psychological needs* will be discussed in the chapter on *early maladaptive schemas*.

To fully understand the power of operant conditioning—how reinforcement is delivered *following* a behavior we produce—we must understand the effect of the amount of the reward, the frequency with which it is received, the duration of the reinforcement, and the schedule on which it is delivered.

Tolerance and Habituation: Psychological and Physiological

When substance abusers are asked, "Why do you do it?" the answer is the same today as it was in 1935: "It makes me feel good!" In behaviorism terms, it is positively reinforcing—a huge R+. Some go into more detail: "If I was tired, it gave me energy; if I was sad, the sadness went away; if I was bored, I found an interest; if I was depressed, it made me happy; if I was anxious, the anxiety went away." Simply stated, they felt better with it than they felt without it.

As we explore the relationship between how reinforcement is delivered and its effects on substance abuse acquisition, it's important to remember that when our substance use first started, some unpleasant feeling state was altered in a positive way. I have had many addicts exclaim that "it was love at first sight!" after they had their first drink or experience with other drugs like speed or heroin. It is very unusual for initial substance use to develop immediately into full-fledged addiction. Clinically, I doubt the assertion and always query patients who usually recant the assertion and admit that it was continued successful removal of an unpleasant affective state that produced addiction. Typically, our first experience is unpleasant: the initial ingestion of nicotine that comes from smoking is accompanied by pain, coughing, and a foul taste in one's mouth. Smoking is a testament to the pain we will endure to resolve some unmet internal need. I continued the painful process of anesthetizing my throat and the cilia in my bronchi, ignoring the taste and the smell, until I could smoke with impunity. Why? Somehow, my smoking transformed me into a tall, slender, debonair movie star à la Michael Rennie. (At least that was my fantasy. And yes, it really does date me!)

The process of addiction is slow and insidious. The initial stages produce pleasure without a lot of negative self-destructive consequences. My initial forays with alcohol resulted in occasionally worshiping at the porcelain throne and some mild discomfort the following day. We learn how to drink in moderation and still obtain the positive emotional effects. Since the effects of alcohol in moderation continue to produce positive emotional states, the drinking is sustained. When the need for those positive emotional states (the removal of a negative emotional state) arises more regularly, we drink more often and thus begin to develop a tolerance for alcohol. As we become habituated to the amount of alcohol we've been consuming, we need more of it to obtain the same emotional state. This is when withdrawal becomes an issue.

At this point, the abuser switches from *psychological homeostasis* to *physiological homeostasis*—avoiding the physical symptoms of withdrawal. With the onset of withdrawal, it becomes necessary to keep small amounts of alcohol in the system at all times in order to avoid it. At this point, the alcohol of choice is typically vodka, as it is relatively odorless, and we can drink it at work and reduce the likelihood that our intoxication will be noticed. Many people select employment that provides them with sufficient autonomy in an environment where substance use may be tolerated and even supported. For example, they get a job as a bartender. It is not uncommon for patrons in a bar to reward the bartender with shots. Restaurants, tattoo parlors, hair salons, and construction sites are all places where substance abuse is common. This is not to imply that the majority of the workers in those environments are substance abusers, only that the tolerance of altered states is elevated.

How many of the alcoholics among us can recount the number of times they drank and vomited their way through Antabuse. Antabuse is an antagonist to alcohol that alcoholics take; it is supposed to keep them from drinking because it makes them violently ill if they drink while taking it. When medical science offered opiate addicts naloxone—a substance that eliminates the effects of opiates—at no cost to them, they were unwilling to take it. Why? The psychological need (the removal of a negative effect) was not met. However, some clinics are more than happy to supply addicts with methadone, which mimics the effects of heroin. The assumption was that it would keep them from using illicit drugs and committing other such crimes in the service of a very expensive addiction. Many heroin addicts are more than willing to tell you that they still use the heroin and sold the methadone to buy it. The point is, whatever drug meets the internal need is the drug a user or abuser will pursue.

Schedules of Reinforcement and Behavioral Maintenance

How reinforcers (the outcomes of our behaviors that bring us pleasure or discomfort) are delivered is through a process called *schedules of reinforcement*. How often a payoff (an R+ or R-) occurs defines the schedule of reinforcement. Reinforcements can be delivered *continuously* (CR); every time you produce the behavior, you are reinforced. Reinforcers can also be delivered on what are called intermittent schedules; these vary in time intervals that are *fixed* or *variable* (F or V). They can also vary in the number (ratio) of responses you have to make to obtain reinforcement, or the interval (I) you have to wait for the reinforcement to be delivered. If you are paid a salary for a week of work, that is a fixed interval (FI) schedule of reinforcement. If you are a car salesperson and are paid only when you can convince someone to purchase a car, you work under a variable ratio (VR) schedule of reinforcement as you do not know how many sales pitches you will have to deliver to make a sale.

The best way to establish a new behavior is through a continuous reinforcement (CR) schedule. That means *every time* you produce the desired behavior, you receive the positive reinforcement R+. When you are young, you have little or no control over the reinforcements you receive. Whatever behaviors are valued by the older people around you—those who supply the reinforcers—are the behaviors you will adopt. In most households, we males were told that big boys do not cry. Later, we were warned, "If you are going to cry, I'll give you something to cry about." These *injunctions—do not feel* and others like it—are the foundations on which later *psychopathology* is based. We will explore *injunctions* (positive and negative rules to live by) in detail in the chapter on *transactional analysis*.

Continuous Reinforcement (CR) Schedule

CRs are the most successful way to establish a behavior, because every time you produce the desired behavior, it is reinforced. There is a reliable connection between *what I do* and *what I get out of it*. This forms not only a strong and predictable synaptic pathway but also a direct connection between substance use and the desired reward. Once established, the best way to maintain a behavior is to employ the types of schedules that deliver fixed, variable, ratio, and interval reinforcements. These are more effective because you have to produce the behavior for a certain amount of time in order to obtain the reinforcement you are seeking. We are willing to work for a week without any primary reinforcements for the secondary reinforcement of money, which we can trade in for primary reinforcements like shelter, food, drugs, and/or alcohol. Unfortunately, active addiction makes it difficult to keep a traditional job because it is not conducive to your altered state and the need to continuously avoid withdrawal. You will begin to trivialize and even dehumanize "worker bees" by referring to them as nine-to-fivers or ham-and-eggers. To justify your behaviors, you will make rationalizations, like, "Why work for nine dollars an hour when one drug deal can get me hundreds or even thousands of dollars—and I can stay stoned while making it?"

A basic parental responsibility is teaching your children and adolescents to *postpone gratification*. When you begin using and abusing substances in early adolescence, you miss this whole process—you don't learn how to deal with difficulties or postpone the gratification of unpleasant emotional states.

The Effect of Fixed and Variable Reinforcement Schedules on Behavior

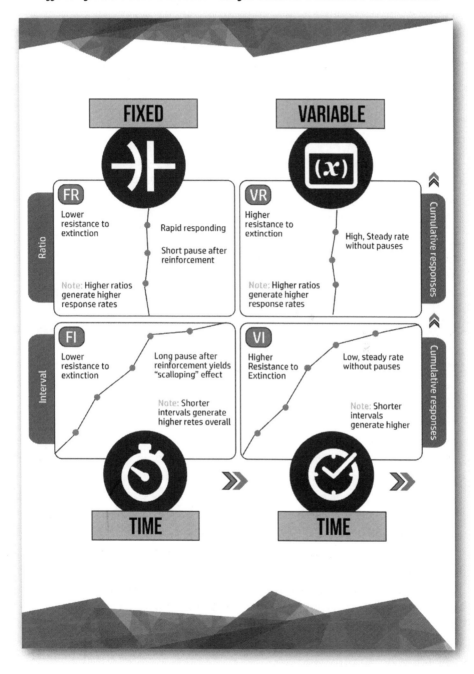

These mixed schedules are particularly important as they relate directly to the self-administration of psychotropic drugs. When you have an unlimited supply of alcohol and your intent is to drink until you pass out, it is completely under your control; this is continuous reinforcement on a VI or VR schedule. When you smoke, the same is true. Both drugs are legal and therefore easy to acquire. This probably explains why they account for over half a million deaths annually. The annual death toll for heroin, cocaine, meth, and other popular psychotropics is collectively around fifty thousand annually. The illicit drugs, on the other hand, are typically more expensive and more difficult to obtain, but they also produce the desired effect of emotional blunting or excitement (depending on the substance), almost instantaneously. Most addicts will opine, "Why ingest or snort it when you can shoot it and have it in your brain almost instantaneously?" Meth is incredibly popular because it costs less and lasts longer than crack cocaine. Look at the resistance to extinction of each schedule.

Modeling, a visual and cognitive method of learning, was proposed and experimentally validated by Albert Bandura in 1986.[78] With this method, we can observe how a particular behavior produces a particular outcome and decide whether we want to emulate that behavior (add that behavior to our repertoire). Modeling is frequently used as a technique for eliminating debilitating behaviors in children. One such experiment used films of children playing with dogs to reduce a child's fear of the animal, which had developed from a previous negative experience with a dog. What does all of this have to do with addiction? One question for those of you who grew up in households where your parents or older siblings *modeled* substance use and abuse for you is whether that may have been one of the contributing factors in your decision to use or abuse substances. That is, did the most influential role models in your life seem to be showing you that substance use was a positive thing? Were angry parents mellower after they sampled their substance of choice? Another question you might ask yourself is whether you felt disenfranchised. Did you not belong to one of the elite groups, like the jocks, preppies, or nerds, and find that there was only one group you could belong to: the *stoners*? Their requirements were not quite as stringent as the others'. The ability to inhale was satisfactory for inclusion. Some of us may have belonged to more than one group, however—an *anomaly* we may want to take a closer look at.

Recall that I took up smoking to emulate a movie star I thought was the epitome of coolness. He was by far the most dashing and debonair individual on the face of the earth. I can still see him standing on the prow of a steamship in his tuxedo, cigarette in hand. My fantasy was that smoking would facilitate my transformation into the same absolute coolness.

All kinds of people are opting to get tattoos earlier in life, and with increasing frequency, as rock stars, professional athletes, and women join the trend. Back in the day, tattoos were the exclusive property of servicemen and members of antisocial subcultures. Ask yourself who your psychological heroes were and what their behaviors were. This may give you some insight into what modeling was all about. Is it any wonder why those who grow up in the hoods or similar environments—where many of the apparently successful are pimps, drug dealers, and other criminals—end up emulating those behaviors? Criminals have the lock on the *secondary reinforcer* (money) that can be traded for all of the *primary reinforcers*.

Eliminating Unwanted Behavior from Your Repertoire

The only way to *eliminate behavior from your repertoire* is to stop producing the undesirable *self-destructive behavior*. More easily said than done, right? Why is that? There are several reasons. So far, we have examined the effect of rewards on the maintenance of behaviors. Rewards work because they signal to our brain that the behavior will produce something we want. When we want to *extinguish* a behavior—especially one on a continuous reinforcement schedule (CR)—we must ascertain that *under no condition* can the inappropriate behavior be reinforced. The problem with that is that *we* control whether that behavior is reinforced. The link between how we have relieved unpleasant states (feeling mad, sad, or scared) or celebrated positive ones has been well established through years of addiction on a *CR schedule that we controlled*—in relieving unpleasantness by altering our brain's chemistry and by introducing *psychotropics* that produce our feelings of pleasure (*R+'s by removing our discomforting R-'s*). So, when we return to the "real world" after completing rehab and experience unpleasant feeling states, our mind and brain already have a well-practiced solution for that. If you know that your brain and mind will resolve the problem without much thought on your part, it is necessary to understand that *only you* can intervene in what seems like an unconscious process by performing some *competing behavior(s)* you learned in rehab. Call your sponsor, pray, or do whatever you learned to do, because the craving (*a learned conditioned response* for dealing with unpleasant feeling states) will pass. It is your awareness that the self-destructive behavior is now under your conscious control that allows you to insert a new *competing behavior* between what was a very maladaptive sequence and the unintended consequences it produced. I know none of you purposely set out to live unmanageable lives. It is, however, the inevitable and unintended outcome of chemically similar addictive substances that interact with the reward systems of the brain.

The relationship among a well-established behavior, substance abuse, and relapse is not so difficult to understand when you recognize how behavior becomes habitual. The more you repeat a behavior, the more you strengthen a synaptic pathway.

One of the most interesting and conversely perplexing facts for the recovering addict is that behavior that has been maintained on a CR schedule with the introduction of *a single positive reinforcement,* or even behavior that has become more or less extinct, can return with a vengeance—and in that case, the old behaviors will become very stable again. Sound familiar? How many times have you experienced an increase in your use after a period of abstinence and sobriety? This is one of those mysteries that seems to call for a biological explanation. (It must be a recurring, relapsing brain disease.) On the contrary, it's simply how the brain works. The more often you repeat a particular behavior, the more that particular synaptic pathway is reinforced. That is how behavior becomes automatic and why it seems to be biologically driven. Because the neural pathway still exists stimuli that were previously associated with it can activate the pathway again. This is where the mind needs to step in and recognize that a competing behavior must be activated to avoid relapse.

All behavior has a purpose, and this fact is critical to our understanding of why we continue to perform behaviors that are self-destructive.

Chapter 4 Glossary

Anomalous process: an explanatory concept in the schema of those observing our behavior, who do not understand that the self-destructive behavior is positively reinforcing to us; behavior they would not engage in—that would interfere with anyone's ability to lead a manageable life—must denote some biological defect in our brain, or an anomalous biological process

Anomaly: something that deviates from what is standard, normal, or expected

Automatic responses: responses that do not require conscious activation because they are well-established parts of our behavioral repertoire

Conditioned response: a stimulus capable of eliciting a response through its repeated pairing with an unconditioned response

Counterintuitive: to an external witness, behavior that can't be understood; behavior with negative consequences that is inexplicably repeated

Extinguish: eliminate a maladaptive behavior from your repertoire

Fixed schedule of reinforcement: the reinforcement comes only on a predetermined basis

Idiosyncratically defined: we, and only we, can decide what positive, negative, neutral, or punishing outcomes our behaviors will produce

Injunctions: the verbal dictates from parents or parental surrogates (i.e., those whose counsel we deem worth listening to) on how to behave, who to be, how to be acknowledged, who establish our worth, and so on; these injunctions can be misconstrued by young children who lack the conceptual tools to make sense of adult verbal or physical behavior

Interval: reinforcement is controlled by the amount of time that has lapsed

Modeling: adding behaviors to your repertoire by observing others and replicating their behavior

Operant conditioning: one of the factors that explains how behaviors are added or subtracted from our repertoire; the effect of the outcome of a behavior on its inclusion in our repertoire

Owning the addiction: accepting full responsibility for your addiction and understanding what has become compulsive behavior

Physiological needs: needs with which we would not continue to survive (e.g., food, water, sleep). To discriminate between wants e.g., " I need a Mink coat".

Postpone gratification: the ability to inhibit one's behavior until an appropriate time for that behavior

Primary reinforcement: a reinforcement (e.g., food, water, or drugs) that has a biological effect on the body's sensors

Psychological needs: a host of perceived needs (safety, security, actualization, recognition etc.)

Psychotropics: chemicals capable of altering the delicate chemistry of the brain

Punishers: negative stimuli that decrease the likelihood that a behavior will be reproduced

R Neutral: an outcome of your behavior that decreases the likelihood that it will be reproduced

R-: replacement of a negative stimulus with a positively reinforcing one; this increases the likelihood that the behavior will be repeated

R+: a response to your behavior that increases the likelihood that it will be repeated

Ratio: the number of responses required to receive a reinforcement and determine its delivery

Reinforcement: the consequence of a behavior you produce either internally or externally; removing an R- positively reinforces an R+ (drinking or using drugs during withdrawal eliminates the *negative* physiological consequences and reinforces addictive behavior).

Repertoire: the complete set of behaviors you are currently capable of producing

Schedules of reinforcement: the relationship between how and when reinforcement is delivered and its effect on the occurrence of the desired behavior

Secondary reinforcers: reinforcers, such as money, that can be used to obtain primary reinforcers

Self-destructive behaviors: behaviors that result in negative outcomes for the person producing them

Stimulus: any event or thing in the environment that we respond to

Triggers (negative): internal or external stimuli that activate existing maladaptive behavioral patterns

Triggers (neutral or positive): anything in the internal or external environment that activates previously learned behavioral sequences

Variable schedule: reinforcement is delivered on a schedule that can change

CHAPTER 5

New Science: Trauma and Early Maladaptive Schemas, yet No Paradigm Shift?

Self-Perception and Behavior: Communicating the Model to the Patient

> *I can't recall exactly when I decided—or believed that I had*
> *discovered—that I was a bad person, but by the time I started*
> *first grade, I saw myself as somehow innately morally defective.*
> —MAIA SZALAVITZ, THE UNBROKEN BRAIN

Trauma, Early Maladaptive Schemas (EMSs), Subpersonalities (SP), and Transactional Analysis (TA): Understanding Internal Dialogue

There is no more powerful demonstration of the ability of a developing mind to extract from the responses of the environment a self-definition, whether good or bad. Maia Szalavitz attributes this realization, in some respect, to the labels that others used to define her.

Self-Perception and Early Maladaptive Schemas Overview

In chapter 5, I will discuss in more detail what I found to be most effective in communicating with people regarding the origin of their self-destructive and maladaptive behavior patterns. It is intended to be complete enough to allow anyone to recognize early maladaptive schemas, psychological games, ego states, and harmful scripts. The discussion of and information regarding early maladaptive schemas is primarily attributed to the work of Jeffrey Young, PhD. Dr. Young comes from the cognitive behavioral school of psychology. I first encountered Dr. Young's *Cognitive Therapy for Personality Disorders: A Schema-Focused Approach* while I was employed as the clinical director of the Stout Street Foundation Inc., a therapeutic community in Denver, Colorado. Most of the residents of this program were dually diagnosed with one or more of the Axis I substance abuse diagnoses as well as one or more of the then-Axis II personality disorders.

I already knew of the difficulty of treating personality disorders, so I was searching for a new approach that might be more effective. I found the implementation of the Young Schema Questionnaire (YSQ) for diagnosis of precipitating conditions to create an explanation that resonated with the residents of the therapeutic community. Transactional analysis theory and feedback helped me communicate to the residents the viability of what we understand to be the source of our executive decision-making function, the frontal and prefrontal cortices. The presentation of EMSs wasn't perceived as psychobabble. Understanding EMSs proved to be most effective in altering the course of their *self-destructive behavior* and allowed them to participate and collaborate in the search for causal factors. The effectiveness of making substance abusers aware of what maladaptive schemas are and, more importantly, the traumatic early environments that were instrumental in creating the maladaptive schemas, became an important tool in making sense out of self-destructive behavior.

If the personality disorder did not exist prior to addiction, many of the characteristics of personality disorders were adopted in service of their addiction(s). The more severe the addiction became in terms of costs (both monetary as well as ethical), the more likely the residents were to have violated legal, moral, and social norms. The very act of attempting to hide the addiction from significant others requires deception. These early attempts to avoid detection places one on the slippery slope of reevaluating one's moral and ethical schemas. Every increase in the severity and extent of the addiction requires the modification of moral and ethical schemas in an antisocial direction. Maladaptive behaviors that were previously unthinkable become viable alternatives in service of the addiction. I've actually considered the option of establishing the validity and reliability of the schema specifically created to deal with addiction. Working with addicts allows insight into the justification systems that are created in service of making their addiction a viable and even prosocial alternative. Unfortunately, or perhaps fortunately, these pretend structures are built on flimsy self-deceptions and are relinquished in the face of rigorous scrutiny.

The schemas posited by Dr. Young have been subjected to empirical verification. They have been found to be statistically valid and reliable. *Valid* means that they represent what they say they represent—internal belief systems that are associated with observable behavior. Someone with a maladaptive schema of mistrust will find it difficult, if not impossible, to trust others. *Reliable* means the test finds the same results each time they test the concept across groups and time. That same person who has a maladaptive schema of mistrust will mistrust others across different situations and in different groups of people.

What are early maladaptive schemas? Schemas are organized systems of knowledge that we have developed through exposure to and experience with not *the* but *our* environment. The distinction between *the environment* and *our environment* is what makes every one of us unique. Monozygotic twins from the same egg have identical DNA, but regardless of that shared DNA, they experience the world differently. What makes their individual worlds different is that they can't both be at the very same place at the very same time, and even if they are at the same place at the same time, when someone is speaking to one twin, he or she is not speaking to the other one. The twins' experiences of the same event are therefore very different. The twin who is not addressed first might ask, "Why did that person address him or her first?"

Remember that as human beings, our very survival depends on creating mental structures that allow us to operate safely, swiftly, and effectively in our world. When our mental structures (software) become filled with inaccurate, misinterpreted, or misconstrued information, the picture of the world we live in becomes distorted.

Recall for a moment what a child could conclude when both of his or her parents work to provide him or her with the events and things they think will make their child's life better. There is no maliciousness in their intent. But what the child experiences is that Mommy and Daddy are not there, so he or she must figure out *why* they're not there. What the child experiences or interprets could be neglect or abandonment, because he or she must make sense out of it. *Since Mommy and Daddy are never wrong and hold all the power in my life,* the child might think, *my assumption is that I must be unworthy, unlovable, or even defective.* Now imagine a life in which this child's mommy and daddy are both home, but they're also both alcoholics and/or drug addicts (addiction is addiction; drug of choice is irrelevant) and physically and emotionally unavailable. Now, imagine what could the child infer from the complete unavailability of their parents?

Imagine for a moment this particular scenario/thought process: *I'm two years old. My diaper is full. My stomach is empty. And Mom and Dad are passed out on the couch. Regardless of what I do, nothing happens. What might I conclude about the likelihood that my needs will be met? That I'm valuable and worthwhile, loved and wanted? That when I am distressed and uncomfortable, someone will be there to help me through the crisis? Or will I conclude that no matter how hard I try to get their attention there is no one out there for me?* These events, though not life threatening, are nonetheless traumatic to the child; they create and confirm solid evidence to prove that his or her pleas for assistance may forever go unanswered.

The information about the lack of concern for the needs of others, that are part of active addiction, is not available to a fourteen-month-old child. Therefore, the ability to place responsibility on the parents for their behavior is also unavailable to the toddler. And so, if it's not a defect in the parent, then it must be a defect in the child, right? That child may wonder, *What is it about me that makes it impossible for Mom and Dad to recognize and respond to my needs?* The need to make sense of the world is relentless; our very survival is dependent upon it. The conclusions that a fourteen-month-old child might arrive at can range from the existential to the pragmatic. At this age, the rudiments of language are beginning to appear. Existentially, is there an "internal knowing" that needs are unlikely to be met, even though he or she can't verbalize that fact?

Our response to the world in these early months following our birth is emotional. At this stage in our development, our primary contact with the world is through our emotions. When our diapers are clean and our bellies are full, we smile. When our diapers are soiled and our stomachs are empty, we cry. If these tears fall on deaf ears when we have no cognitive skills to make sense of it, what might we conclude? Children who are raised in nonresponsive environments—where parents lack the skills or emotional health to adequately nurture their children—are typically afflicted with a medical condition called failure to thrive (FTT). FTT children are typically on the very low end of the height and weight scales. When it's a medical condition, the causes are typically related to diet and nutrition and are treatable. When it's emotional, it goes untreated and potentially becomes an EMS.

There are numerous ways that EMSs can form. It is important to understand that many maladaptive schemas are the result of unintended outcomes. Take again, for example, the working parents who are neither intentionally distant nor unloving; they are simply tired after a hard day's work. Think about the situation in which someone else in the family is chronically ill or disabled, someone who requires as much or more attention than the two-year-old. What kinds of schemas are developed when you're raised in a crime family where substance use and abuse is introduced by your parents and legal and social norm violation is not only sanctioned but applauded? What kind of schemas are you going to develop regarding prosocial behavior? What if you are physically, sexually, and/or psychologically abused and told that you are stupid, dirty, or unworthy? What if you are over- or underweight? Too tall or too short? Too poor? Smart? Not particularly good at sports? What if you have acne or a learning disability? What if your parents dress you funny—or are rich and provide you with every conceivable toy? There are no two individuals who experience the world in exactly the same way. To determine the source of the EMS, an accurate, dispassionately acquired history (without critical comment about caregivers) must be obtained. As adults, we have a tendency to forgive and forget. I frequently hear, "I love my mom and dad, despite the fact that they were horrible parents" and "they did the best they could with what they had."

It is critical to understand that the purpose of getting an accurate picture of the world that *you* grew up in will help you see what the conditions were that allowed you to draw conclusions about yourself that were inaccurate. The purpose is not to blame anyone but to understand what environment you were trying to make sense of and understand. When you understand that the negative conclusions you drew about yourself were *unintended consequences* created by an undeveloped mind, you're making progress. When you have the luxury of viewing the environment that you were subjected to with the cognitive skills of a grown-up, you can begin to understand why you drew those negative conclusions about yourself and then begin to reevaluate them. These negative conclusions are at the root of your maladaptive schemas and self-destructive behavior. If that assertion is correct and the maladaptive schemas were never addressed, it's no wonder that you continued to hurt yourself with relapse after relapse. Without knowing what was broken and how it was broken, it is impossible to fix it; it was not a "lack of moral fiber" on your part. If this explanation strikes a resonant chord with you, I would recommend that you find a cognitive behavioral therapist who has the skills to address your early maladaptive schemas and help you work through them.

I, as a therapist, listen to you as you describe yourself, and you tell me who and what you think you are, have been, and always will be. From this discussion, I'm able to determine what *your existential position is*. Your existential position is your perception of yourself that you presume is cast in stone. When you describe yourself as an alcoholic or an addict, it is a description of *I was, have been, am now, and always will be.* If you believe that *what I am is what I think I am*, how profitable is it to describe yourself as an alcoholic or an addict? What are the implications of that self-description? I understand that the purpose of identifying yourself in that way for AA and NA is to remind you that you *had* (past tense) allowed your life to become unmanageable by depending upon alcohol and/or drugs to *manage the way you felt* until you reached the point of physical addiction. At that point, you had to choose either to avoid withdrawal and continue to use or quit using.

At the time, it seemed far easier to continue to use rather than go through the discomfort of withdrawal. AA and NA believe the grandiosity of thinking that you are cured is the slippery slope that allows you to think you could use just one more time and control it. When you have spent the majority of your life managing your feelings by manipulating your neurotransmitters, it's stupid to think that your mind/brain doesn't remember how much easier it is to pop a pill or have a drink than go through the arduous task of figuring out what it is that leads you into unpleasant thinking and feeling that makes a life-and-death decision a viable option.

In the short term, it is an appropriate caveat, regarding a few weeks, a few months, or even a few years of sobriety. I would much prefer that you acknowledge to yourself that in the not-too-distant past you lacked sufficient reality testing, not moral fiber, to acknowledge that you were risking your life with substance use.

After twenty years without cigarettes, I no longer consider myself a smoker; I wouldn't take one if you offered it to me, regardless of how bad I might feel. I did not resume smoking following the most traumatic event of my life: the death of my daughter. I did revert to aggressively acting out in response to what I considered inappropriate incursions on my physical and psychological space. By the same token, I will not accept a cigar to celebrate the birth of your offspring—not even a marvelous Cuban. Despite the fact that it's been twenty years, my mind and brain remember the brief respite from whatever was bothering me that was provided by the nicotine. Why take a chance?

It is important to remember that our beliefs about substance dependence are nothing more than a schema based on whatever beliefs we hold. Those beliefs will dictate our behavior when it comes to notions about the possibility of our sustained sobriety and "cure." Make no mistake: if I believe I am biologically defective, I will behave in accordance with that belief. If I hold that belief, relapse simply becomes a part of recovery, rather than a choice I make at that point in time to alter the way I feel. The "disease" made me do it. I had no choice in the matter. The "disease" wouldn't let me call my sponsor or a friend, pray, or smoke a cigarette for only the seven minutes the craving lasted. Really!

Existential Positions; The "OK Corral"

IOK

+ - Get Rid of I Am OK+ and You Are Not-	+ + Get On with I Am OK + and You Are OK+
- - Get Nowhere with I Am Not OK- and You Are Not OK-	- + Get Away from I Am Not OK- and You Are OK+

YNOK YOK

INOK

The origin of early maladaptive schemas and existential positions is based on the schemas that we believe define us. If the schemas we use to define the self are negative (I am an addict; a bad son, daughter, father, mother, or grandchild; a thief; an abuser; uneducated; stupid; a dropout; voted most likely not to succeed; not lovable; not deserving of love; abandoned; neglected; or physically/emotionally/sexually abused), it's all because of something I did; it's what I had coming. What is not realized is that the order is reversed. You *became* those things *because* that's what you *believe* you had coming as opposed to what you were born to be. Do you honestly think you were biologically ordained, as a child, to live an unmanageable life?

For the spiritual or religious among you, higher powers "don't make no junk!" At this point, we will explore existential positions that we may integrate them with early maladaptive schemas. We'll explore this in more detail in the section on subpersonalities and transactional analysis (TA).

Dr. Franklin Ernst was a practicing psychiatrist who became aware of the work of Dr. Eric Berne.[79] Dr. Ernst studied with Dr. Berne and became one of the founding and teaching members of the International Transactional Analysis Association (ITAA). One of his major contributions to theory and practice was the construction of what he called the OK Corral. You can see from the diagram that there are four coordinates that are created by the OK or not OK (NOK) relationships between two people. Each of the positions in the OK Corral is associated with beliefs and expectations about how interactions with other people will go. Each of these life positions is like a schema representing your existential position in life. In the first position, I see myself as IOK (I Am OK), and I see you as YOK (You Are OK). This is the "get-on-with-it" position (GOW). In this position, there's no reason to play games producing either a positive or negative outcome; neither of us is at risk in this transaction.

Let me move to the secondary position, where I think I'm OK (IOK), but I think the person I'm dealing with is not OK (NOK); my ultimate purpose is to remove them from my space. This is the "get-rid-of" position (GRO). If they need a negative payoff from someone who sees them as not OK (NOK), then the easiest thing to do is engage that person and set them up to reject you. If, on the other hand, you find yourself in the position where you're not OK (NOK), and you believe the other person is OK (OK), the best way not to suffer any negative feelings about yourself is to "get away from" (GAF) that person. The fourth position is one that places you in rather dire straits. When you believe that you are not OK (NOK) and that the people around you are not OK (NOK), the best solution is to withdraw. It is the most dangerous position because the next step is I'm NOK, you're NOK, and this space is NOK—meaning the world is not OK. This position is "helpless and hopeless," which makes us question whether it's reasonable to even remain alive. This is the position people are in when they attempt to or do commit suicide. Early maladaptive schemas are part and parcel of the existential positions that each of us holds. To test yours, go to http://lifetraptest.com/ and select *Test Your Life Trap*.

Early Maladaptive Schemas Described

Dr. Jeffery Young has reliably demonstrated the existence of eighteen maladaptive schemas. What that means is that these maladaptive schemas are not a figment of his imagination but are instead a description of our thought processes that can and will predict a person's behavioral response to incoming stimuli from the world around him or her. The schemas are, to borrow words, "truths we hold to be self-evident." That is, they are the world from our idiosyncratic point of view. If you find disclosing your EMSs uncomfortable and attempt to keep them from your treating professional, you are only tricking yourself. You can contact a cognitive behavioral psychologist, social worker, or psychiatrist, or the Schema Therapy Institutes in New York or New Jersey, to find a cognitive behavioral therapist who has been trained to deal with these maladaptive schemas. Ask them what they know about ACEs and EMSs specifically. You are purchasing a treatment product!

Remember, it is continuing to hold on to these negative beliefs about yourself that is at the root of your self-destructive behavior. Your willingness to face them, embrace them, and modify them in such a way as to live the bountiful life that you deserve is the reason you're reading this.

The maladaptive schemas are grouped by clusters. What that means is that several of the maladaptive schemas are like cousins: they are different but definitely related. They are self-perceptions that were created by a particular group of similar traumatic experiences. The following descriptions are my interpretation of Dr. Young's early maladaptive schemas; he does not grant permission to reprint his work. I will remain as close to his descriptions as possible. However, this provides me with the opportunity to integrate concepts from transactional analysis and subpersonalities with the early maladaptive schemas, and that may provide a more robust conceptual framework.

Disconnection and Rejection

Disconnection and rejection is a reference to our perception that for some reason, we are not worthy of receiving those things that Abraham Maslow described as the foundation of needs necessary to become a fully "actualized person": safety, security, love, empathy, nurturing, the ability to share your feelings and have them acknowledged, spontaneity, social belonging, praise, respect, and the like.[80] These needs were not met. Bessel van der Kolk discusses the psycho-physiological correlates related to normal development and how trauma disrupts the normal development by freezing compensatory processes in time. These theories predict the basic I Am Not OK position in the OK Corral Ask yourself what kind of early environment would leave a young child with this kind of a belief system regarding their worth.

In their early environment basic needs would probably be ignored, lack of awareness of their feelings or their importance, rejection or withholding of affection is certainly critical and very likely abusive. If you are incapable of recognizing that you're dealing with a young child, how can you appropriately tend to their needs? If birds of a feather flock together, their peers will feel the same way about themselves. They will typically be withdrawn, isolated, or isolating, and not feel like they belong. The maladaptive schemas typically associated with this environment are *emotional deprivation, mistrust/abuse, emotional inhibition, defectiveness/shame,* and *social isolation/ alienation.*

Emotional deprivation: the expectation one desires for a normal degree of emotional support from others will not be adequately met by others. Dr. Young posits three major forms of deprivation:

- **Deprivation of nurturance:** *I will not receive much attention or experience much companionship from peers or significant others, or expect to be treated warmly.*
- **Deprivation of empathy:** *If, as a child, my feelings have thus far been unimportant, how can I be cheated, manipulated, and taken advantage of as I age and expect my feelings to be important? If I was not understood at home, why would I expect to be understood now? If my caregivers didn't listen then, why would anyone listen to me now? If my feelings were not accepted as important then, why would my feelings be important now? I have already been taught that what's going on inside of me is not important.*
- **Deprivation of guidance and protection:** *If the environment I was in did not allow me to think that I would be protected and guided by those who had my best interests at heart, why would I expect it to change? How did I acquire strength and self-confidence in that environment?*

Mistrust/abuse: *My willingness to believe that my environment is safe is predicated on whether it was safe. If I was physically harmed, abused, sexually abused, told that they wouldn't be there for me, do things with me, or I was humiliated or taken advantage of, why would I trust now? Unfortunately, the harm is perceived as intentional and related to something I did, which means that I deserve the harmful treatment I am receiving. This may create the expectation that I will always be mistreated. This sets in motion a series of behaviors that will force others to react to me and give me the outcome that I expect, which validates my doubt that I have anything good coming.*

Emotional inhibition: *My willingness to be emotionally spontaneous is rigidly controlled. I fear the negative consequences of freely sharing what I feel.* This is a typical strategy for avoiding the disapproval of others. The underlying assumption of this emotional inhibition is predicated on feelings of guilt and shame and a lack of self-worth. (*I often fear that if I express what I'm feeling, I may lose control.*) Several common expressions of inhibition are as follows:

- no internal belief that you have permission to express your anger or aggressive thoughts

- discomfort in showing affection and love for fear that it will be misinterpreted or not accepted
- an unwillingness to share your private thoughts and feelings for fear they will generally not be accepted and may even be criticized by the person with whom you're sharing them
- excessive emotional control of spontaneous behavior (joy, sexual excitement, play, etc.)
- avoiding intimacy by not expressing your vulnerability or communicating your feelings and needs to others
- excluding the spontaneous part of your personality and rigidly adhering to "adult" or rational behavior while disregarding your emotions; your family of origin typically failed to respond appropriately to your expression of emotion (they may have told you, "Don't cry, or I'll give you something to cry about!" or "children are to be seen and not heard").

Defectiveness/shame: this schema is particularly debilitating because you assume that you are basically defective and is accompanied by feelings of unworthiness and fears that you are unwanted or inferior in important ways. The most important aspect of this belief is the fear that if this defect became public, your rejection by everyone would be complete. Imagine the life of a leper, who is treated as untouchable, shunned by all, and deported to a leper colony. When you harbor this fear of discovery, it is critical to hide your defect. Criticism must be avoided at all costs; rejection must be avoided too. You cling to justifications, to any defense that will help avoid discovery or exposure of your defect. Until or unless your perceived defect is discovered, you must be on guard to defend any assertion that you are less than perfect. Once again, intimacy must be avoided at all costs. Insecurity around others or a sense of shame regarding one's perceived flaws can produce strategies to avoid scrutiny. These flaws may be private (e.g., selfishness, angry impulses, and unacceptable sexual desires) or public (e.g., an unattractive physical appearance and social awkwardness). Typical family of origin was hypercritical about some or all of your abilities, continually compared you to a sibling or others, found you wanting, and focused on what they perceived as a physical defect (you were too fat or too thin, your nose was too big, or your ears stuck out).

Social isolation/alienation: the perception or belief that you don't belong with the rest of the world, are somehow different from other people, and are not part of any group or community is a form of social isolation. This belief system may produce the sense that one is a social, physical, or intellectual outcast who doesn't fit in or who has been excluded by a group, community, or the world at large.

Impaired Autonomy and Performance

This belief system is created by perceptions of one's own competence. Competence is based on one's perception of self: *I am capable of performing independently.* The expectation may extend to the belief that there are forces at work in the environment that will limit your ability to be successful. This expectation can extend to the belief that one lacks adequate support from others in the environment. With such a lack of confidence, the world can be a very dangerous place. Visualize a family environment where the child is overprotected and not allowed the opportunity to explore or try different things out of parental fear that harm could come to the child—where the parent does everything for the child, tells him or her what to think and feel, dictates the appropriate emotional response, and so on. How does one develop self-confidence without being able to act on his or her own and evaluate the consequences of his or her behaviors? Typical family of origin undermines the child's self-confidence. They are overprotective, enmeshed, failing to reward success, highly controlling, focused inordinately on unrealistic dangers, and invalidating when the child expresses his or her own needs and feelings. This particular set of maladaptive schemas produces *dependence/incompetence, abandonment/instability, vulnerability to harm or illness, enmeshment/undeveloped self, failure,* and *subjugation* or *invalidation.*

Dependence/incompetence: the belief that one is incapable of functioning independently to complete everyday responsibilities without considerable support or help without the assistance of others. The fear of tackling a new task is that one will not be able to complete the task to some imagined other's satisfaction (typically a parent), or make a decision without input from someone who may criticize the decision, and so on.

Abandonment/instability: an irrational and exaggerated fear that the people one relies on most for security, connection, and help will suddenly abandon one forever. There are concerns that they will abandon you for extended periods of time and not be available for you when you think you need them. The belief that your emotional stability, coupled with your fear of abandonment, will impede your ability to function and your surviving life without the assistance of "significant others."

This often involves the expectation that those you rely on will not be available to provide emotional support, strength, or protection on a consistent, ongoing basis. This fear of abandonment creates the perception in others that you may be emotionally unstable, unpredictable, unreliable, and not consistently available. Think about what must have gone on at the home of the family origin. Sometimes, they were available to meet your needs, but the next time, they were unavailable; this left you with the belief that emotional support was unpredictable. That does not imply malicious behavior on anyone's part but could include parents with similar beliefs, illness, or unavailability due to their addiction, and so on.

Vulnerability to harm or illness: this is the "external-locus-of-control" position where one believes that he or she is the victim of circumstances, most of which are beyond their control.[81] One's ability to mitigate an unexpected catastrophe is impaired or nonexistent. Fears are focused on a variety of categories, including the following:

- medical (stroke or heart attack)
- emotional catastrophes (emotional breakdowns or the inability to control emotions)
- external catastrophes (being victimized by criminals, hurricanes, tornadoes, vehicular accidents, elevators malfunctioning, airplane crashes, or earthquakes)
- family of origin is reinforcing the belief that the world isn't a safe place; catastrophizing frequently; an actual traumatic event of sufficient magnitude that it produced a posttraumatic stress disorder (PTSD)

Enmeshment/undeveloped self: enmeshment with another individual is pathological; enmeshment exists when the boundaries between caregivers and the person they're giving care to are limited or nonexistent. The caregivers receive their "OK-ness" by thinking and doing everything they possibly can for the person in their care. No boundaries are established, and the person they are caring for is not allowed to suffer the consequences of his or her behaviors. A real-life example of this pathological relationship between caregivers and their charges has resulted in a new defense for inappropriate behavior described and argued in court as "affluenza."[82] A sixteen-year-old boy from a very wealthy family drove while drunk and killed four people. This was not his first drunk-driving offense. The consequence for his behavior was to be placed in a high-end treatment program. The most recent development in this case is that his mother helped him flee to Mexico after a social media post showed him at a party where alcohol was being consumed—a violation of his probation that could have resulted in actual incarceration. This excessive emotional involvement and closeness with one or more significant others (usually parents or partners) occurs at the expense of full individuation or normal social development. This often involves the feeling that one or both of the enmeshed individuals will not survive or have a reason to live without the constant involvement of the other.

At some level, some individuals recognize that this level of over involvement from the caregiver or partner in their life is pathological and not in their best interest. They do define the relationship as intrusive, lacking in appropriate boundaries, smothering, and so on. There are recriminations from the caregiver, who wishes to maintain the relationship and wants to know why you won't accept his or her "love." Because they're not allowed to make their own decisions about how to run their lives, many feel rudderless and guilty for not accepting the love that is offered.

Failure: the internal belief system that one is a total loser; the belief that one is now, has been, and will always be a failure. The failure syndrome can be localized (I can't seem to keep a job) or generalized (I'm no good at anything and worse than everyone). Typically, this belief system is inculcated early in life. It can be the result of comparisons to older siblings, age-appropriate peers, or people in general. This person endures constant comparisons to others who are succeeding, criticism for not trying hard enough, and affirmations that he or she is inept and unable and always will be. This is distinguished from defectiveness because the belief in ones inadequacy is driven primarily by one's sense of achievement and success, rather than on social competence.

Subjugation/invalidation: *The other person's needs and wants are more important than mine.* Other people's needs come first. This is manifested by never asking for what you want and never making a decision about what the group would do, even if asked. The belief is they would ignore the option if you presented it. This is predicated on the perception that your wants and feelings were not responded to in the early environment. The expression of your thoughts and feelings would be criticized or result in your abandonment. There is a subjugation of needs: suppression of one's legitimate preferences rights, needs, and desires. This can also feature an invalidation or suppression of one's emotions because of the expectation that one's feelings will be discounted, ignored, criticized, or not taken seriously by others or that there will be some kind of punishment or rejection by others for expressing one's emotions.

This position is described in TA terms as over adaptation. Being over adapted is aptly described as being a person who "wouldn't say *shit* if they had a mouthful." This schema frequently presents as excessive compliance combined with hypersensitivity to feeling trapped or controlled. It often leads to "stamp collecting," in which the person swallows insults and discounts his or her own worth and feelings. When enough stamps have been collected, you deserve relief in the form of whatever your heart desires. Essentially, the internal dialogue becomes, I have been hurt or have discounted enough that now it's my turn to strike out physically, drink, use drugs, use passive aggression, withdraw my affection, punish, or manifest physical symptoms that will result in their feeling guilty if they don't do your bidding. These inappropriate expressions of your hurt are obviously maladaptive.

Impaired Limits

That case of "affluenza" has implications here as well. The control of our public behavior is determined by several factors. One factor is whether we view our behavior as internally or externally controlled. An internal-locus-of-control orientation places responsibility on us to make a decision about how we are going to respond. An external locus of control means that our response to others will be controlled by what others do to us. When you say, "You made me do it" or "I didn't have a choice," you really mean, "You are responsible for my response to you." *It was simply a reflexive behavior,* you rationalize, *as opposed to a choice on my part.* These rationalizations are indications of an external-locus-of-control belief system and represent an unwillingness to accept responsibility for and review the consequences of our behavior before we omit it. There is no requirement for impulse control. The absence of a belief that behavior is predicated on a decision as opposed to a knee-jerk reaction determines whether our limits are impaired. What this looks like behaviorally is difficulty respecting the rights of others or cooperating with others, making commitments, controlling one's emotions and impulses, or setting and meeting realistic personal goals. Impaired limits have several faces: some brag or present themselves as "all that and a bag of chips." Some of these individuals are entitled or self-aggrandizing while others may behave in an impulsive and an undisciplined manner. The typical family of origin is the "affluenza family," parents who were so wealthy that the defendant never learned appropriate internal controls because his family never taught or required accountability for his behavior. The family was characterized by over permissiveness, a lack of boundaries, overindulgence, the failure to enforce normal rules, and the conveyance of a sense of superiority relative to other people. Parents typically do not provide sufficient confrontation, discipline, negative consequences, and limit-setting relating to taking responsibility, cooperating in a reciprocal manner, restraining impulses, sticking to a task, following social rules, and postponing short-term gratification in order to obtain long-term goals. In some cases, the child may not have been expected to tolerate normal levels of discomfort or may not have received adequate supervision, direction, or guidance. The early maladaptive schemas developing from this environment can produce *entitlement/grandiosity and/or insufficient self-control/self-discipline.*

Entitlement/grandiosity: "I deserve whatever I want or do because I'm special, more deserving, and better than you. Which part of that do you not understand?" That is the feeling that one is superior to other people, entitled to special rights and privileges, or not bound by the rules of reciprocity that guide normal social interactions. This often involves an insistence that one should be able to do or have whatever one wants, regardless of what is realistic, what others consider reasonable and socially acceptable, or the harm done to others. The belief in one's superiority allows and permits one to present as the most competent, successful, or valuable, and so on. Self-permission is given to be the best, regardless of the cost to others. Social situations are strictly to present why their self-aggrandizement is so well deserved. While we examined "My needs come last" in the failure schema, this schema is the opposite: "My needs come first." Relationships are maintained to support this delusion. The relationships are symbiotic because the grandiose one has a fan club, and those who discount themselves get to hobnob with the delusional Mr. or Mrs. Successful.

Insufficient self-control/self-discipline: this schema is recognized by what appears to be an inability—as opposed to the unwillingness—to express behaviors, feelings, and emotions at an appropriate time and in an appropriate place. This is the kind of behavior that we refuse to tolerate from children as they age. Postponement of immediate gratification is a requirement of successful socialization. This impulsivity presents as insufficient self-control, discipline frustration tolerance, and need for immediate gratification. While this may appear to be or present as ADD or ADHD, it is not a biological disorder. Instead, it is a psychological disorder, and careful observation will distinguish between the two. These individuals really believe they are unable to control these impulses. This may present as difficulty staying focused on one task, especially if it is boring or unpleasant, regardless of the long-term benefits. This is a frequent excuse used in addictive populations where the biological disorder prohibits users from abstaining: "What do you expect from a guy/gal with a biological disease?"

Excessive Responsibility and Standards

This maladaptive schema of excessive responsibility and standards is generated in part by the grandiosity that everything that is wrong is your fault or was caused by you. The solution to resolving your guilt and reducing your self-castigation is met by meeting excessively strict internalized rules and expectations in most aspects of your life. This presents as very rigid, orderly, and overadaptive adherence to perceived rules and expectations of others. Typically, this requires suppression of one's own feelings and emotions and the expression of their preferences. This is also typified by the belief that "my needs are the least important, and they probably come last." This family of origin is rigid, authoritarian, demanding, and tyrannical, and frequently punitive standards that are set are not met. Postponement of gratification is a critical factor in behaviors that are to be described as appropriate.

The stereotypes presented in social media are excessive paternal control with incredibly high standards expected, typically in ministerial or military (including law-enforcement) families with extremely low self-esteem. They act in the hope that the appearance of rigid social control will elevate their social status. Children may be expected to sacrifice their own needs most of the time to take care of others. An unwillingness to adapt to this expectation may result in feelings of guilt, shame, or selfishness when engaging in positive or enjoyable activities that could result in physical punishment. For oneself, meeting responsibilities, a pursuit of perfectionism, an obsession to take care of other people at the expense of oneself, a rigid adherence to ethical and moral principles and following rules, stoicism, and avoiding mistakes take precedent over pleasure, joy, and relaxation. It is not uncommon for these persons to attempt to inflict their excessively high standards on others and criticize them for not complying under the guise of "I'm only trying to help you." Some individuals expect others to meet their own unrealistically demanding sense of responsibility and standards. The early maladaptive schemas that can form from this environment are *self-sacrifice, unrelenting standards/hypercriticalness, approval seeking/recognition seeking, negativity/pessimism*, and *self-punitiveness*.

Self-Sacrifice: I find this schema frequently in the addictive population: "Other people's feelings and needs are more important than mine." Typically, an excessive focus on voluntarily meeting the needs of others is exhibited. The most common reasons are: to prevent causing pain to others, to avoid guilt and feeling selfish, or to maintain the connections with others perceived as needier. Mind-numbing substances allow them to ignore the admonition that they must be self-sacrificing, or the schema relieves them of guilt and shame. This often results from high standards related to over responsibility to others, regardless of the cost to oneself. This can be the very real, pervasive situation where someone was very ill, and the situation actually required self-monitoring and self-sacrifice. This creates a real sensitivity to the pain of others or from an implicit belief that taking care of others is morally or ethically more important than self-care. This can produce the awareness that one's own needs are not being adequately met, and it can lead to resentment toward those who are being taking care of.

Unrelenting standards/hyper-criticalness: from the OK Corral perspective, the schema is based upon the belief that "I will only be OK when I am perfect and everything around me is perfect." Standards are typically unrealistically high, and perfection is a standard. The same set of standards is expected for those around them. To fail to meet the standards results in anxiety, self-castigation, guilt, and shame that one is not good enough and has let down those whom the person allows to set standards for them. Relaxation, play, and postponement of gratification are frequently not an option. Unrelenting standards are typically presented with (a) perfectionism, inordinate attention to detail, or an underestimation of how good one's own performances are relative to the norm; (b) rigid rules and authoritarian absolutes featuring terms such as *should, shouldn't, have to, must,* and *mustn't* in many areas of life, such as unrealistically high moral, ethical, cultural, or religious principles and a preoccupation with time and efficiency, so that more can be accomplished; or (c) a sense of being driven to accomplish and achieve at a very high level, often across many areas of life.

Approval-Seeking/recognition-seeking: this position in the OK Corral is also based on the premise that "I will be OK when the people I perceive as OK tell me I'm OK." This position is also defined by an excessive emphasis on gaining approval, recognition, or attention from other people, or fitting in, at the expense of developing a secure and true sense of self. Self is defined primarily by the reactions of others to one's behaviors, rather than one's own natural inclinations. This sometimes includes an overemphasis on obtaining social status and acceptance by striving to obtain the accoutrements of the group from which you are seeking approval. In socially appropriate situations, it's: "I can be the top salesman of legal goods." In the criminal subculture, it's: "I can cook the most meth, establish the largest crew, and drive the most expensive car." Status, however defined, is the primary goal. Appearance, social acceptance, money, or achievement are desired in order to gain approval, admiration, or attention (not primarily for power control). It also often includes high awareness of what the group you're seeking recognition from will approve of and a willingness to change yourself accordingly. This frequently results in major life decisions that are inauthentic or unsatisfying, or in hypersensitivity to rejection.

Negativity/pessimism: this position in the OK Corral is a pervasive, lifelong focus on the negative aspects of life. It is the position which is compounded because not only am I "not OK; but *the entire world* is not OK!" Imagine a worldview that suggests that every glass is half empty—that Murphy's Law was written for you, so anything bad that *can* happen *will* happen. This is classic catastrophizing. This expectation is pervasive across every area of life. Life for you is one catastrophe followed by another. People are untrustworthy and will betray you. Those you care about will disappoint, betray, or abandon you. At the extremes of this life position are expectations that a headache is the harbinger of brain cancer. Pessimism invades all aspects of your life (financial, social, medical, biological, spiritual, and so on). Remember that the maintenance of schemas depends upon reclassifying events that are inconsistent with your schema as anomalies. If something good happens in any aspect of your life, it is because things are going to be different. Better was simply a minor perturbation in the universe and does not portend that things will improve.. You may say, "If it's not bad now, it will be soon." This position minimizes risk-taking and supports the belief that you have no control over what happens to you. This is the typical external-locus-of-control position. One is always to be acted upon by events beyond your control. This is a life filled with catastrophizing, focusing on and anticipating what and how things in my life will disintegrate. Because you do not trust that the decisions you make will have positive outcomes, this is a very difficult way to live.

Punitiveness: this schema is not appreciably different than the others in the "I'm not OK" life position. The way in which it differs is characterized by these individuals believe they should be treated because of the way they are not OK. Their belief is that they deserve severe punishment for anything they do wrong. The belief is that anger, intolerance, and impatience for failure to meet some standards (which may be unrealistic and excessively high) should be met punitively. This behavior usually mimics the response that was meted out by caregivers or significant others regarding their performance. If mistakes weren't allowed in their household, you don't allow them in yours. If there were no extenuating circumstances acknowledged for mistakes you made, you don't allow them in others. A rigid and authoritarian set of expectations that you and they must comply with your standards is what typifies this schema. There are no acceptable excuses for behavior that doesn't meet your standards. In communication with others around you, this is typically the vocabulary tone of voice that you received. When a parent or parental surrogate castigates you, the feeling you're left with is that you deserve the punishment, their contemptuous degrading and humiliating comments they use describing you. There is little or no concern for your feelings, as their goal is to obtain your rigid adherence to their demands. Individuals typically demonstrate a tone of voice or behavior that is degrading, contemptuous, or demeaning toward the person to be deserving of punishment, including themselves. The internal dialogue (self-talk) is hypercritical and intropunitive. There is no better place to observe this self-punitive behavior than at competitive sporting events. What do you say to yourself when you shank a drive, strike out, drop a pass, or misspell a word?

The descriptions of the maladaptive schemas will allow you to answer the question, "Do any of these self-perceptions, belief systems, or schemas that I hold about myself and my life sound and feel familiar?" There's a branch of psychology in the treatment community that specifically treats these cognitive belief systems. You can find specialists in this field by contacting the Schema Therapy Institute (*www.schematherapy.com*) headed by Dr. Young in New York.

If you are seriously seeking assistance with your self-destructive behavior and have not been exposed to AA, NA or the principles behind the "twelve steps" in The Principle Approach by Dr. David Sutton,[83] then you may not understand that treatment begins with the admission that the skills you currently possess are inadequate to provide you with the tools you need to modify your behavior. Rigorous honesty is the requirement. Hiding those elements of your life and behavior that you are ashamed of will simply keep you enmeshed in your maladaptive schemas. I acknowledge that there are thousands, perhaps millions of people who were once addicted who have made the decision to stop using by themselves and are successfully living non-addictive lives.

This treatment approach is based on the assumption that the conclusions you drew about yourself because of the environment that you were raised in can and must be reinterpreted in order for you to stop treating yourself badly. One of the statements AA relies on is *your secrets will keep you sick*. Until you are rigorously honest with yourself and others, you will continue to consider yourself worse off than pond scum, or as I often put it, lower than whale poop.

Strategies for Maintaining and/or Adapting to Your Maladaptive Schemas

From our initial discussion of schemas, it's critical to remember that once EMSs are established, we will do our very best to maintain them. Remember in our initial discussion one of the most important characteristics of schemas is that any information that is contradictory or does not fit into the schema must be discounted, ignored, or modified in some way so that we don't have to give up the schema or alter it in any way. Dr. Young describes three basic coping styles that we adopt with respect to our schemas.

His first coping style is called *surrender*. As a description, surrender suggests the response to the maladaptive schema is to accept it and find ways to perpetuate it. Accepting it means that we must engage in activities with the people around us who will provide us with the feedback that our beliefs about ourselves are in fact accurate. Therefore "surrenderers" are passive and submissive. They will do what they can to avoid conflict and please people. They will behave in ways that will obtain the feedback that validates their beliefs about themselves. Contradictory data is viewed as either anomalous or erroneous.

The second coping style is *avoidance*. As the name implies, the strategy with this coping style is to figure out how to avoid acknowledging the schema entirely. This is perhaps the most prevalent style that I see among addicts. The first of the strategies of this coping style are called social withdrawal and excessive autonomy. These strategies find ways to avoid *interacting* with the world. This is perhaps a strategy of relying on an inordinate focus on independence and self-reliance rather than involvement with others—avoiding others through private activities such as self-absorption in television, reading, computers, computer gaming, solitary work, and so on. The second technique of avoidance is called *compulsive stimulation seeking*. As the name implies, activities such as bodybuilding, gambling, risk-taking, sex, or shopping are engaged in on a compulsive basis. The third strategy is called *addictive self-soothing*, and it is one of the most prevalent among addicts. As the name implies, dealing is completely avoided through addictions. Alterations in the brain chemistry through alcohol and drugs and other compulsive behaviors such as overeating or excessive masturbation are common. The last avoidant technique is called *psychological withdrawal*. Psychological withdrawal is characterized by many of the psychological techniques we have, such as isolation, denial, intellectualization, dissociation, and fantasy. The third coping style is called *counterattack* or *overcompensation*.

- *Aggression/hostility* is a strategy whereby we externalize our negative feelings about ourselves by attacking others through criticism, defiance, abuse, blame, and so on.
- *Dominance* or *excessive self-assertion* is essentially forcing others to bend to your will, demonstrating your worth at their expense.
- *Recognition-seeking/status-seeking* allows one to feel better about oneself and avoid dealing with the negative maladaptive schema by impressing others, achieving as much as you possibly can, increasing your status through monetary or other accomplishments, and incessant attention seeking.
- *Manipulation/exploitation* is a strategy employed by individuals with conduct and personality disorders who either overtly or covertly manipulate, seduce, con, and so on.
- *Passive-aggressive* or *rebellious behavior* is typically a covert strategy wherein noncompliance is accomplished by avoidant/covert techniques like pouting, procrastinating, poor performance, tardiness, childish strategies, and excuses.
- *Excessive orderliness/obsessionality* is the "be perfect" strategy whereby most behavior has an obsessive quality to it. Behavior is rigid (and can't be deviated from), orderly, well planned, and lacking in spontaneity.

These are the strategies for dealing with our EMSs. Once again, if you recognize yourself in these descriptions, there are competent, well-trained cognitive behavioral therapists who can help you deal with these issues.

CHAPTER 6

Subpersonalities (SPs) and Transactional Analysis (TA)

Subpersonalities

The term subpersonalities was popularized by John in; Subpersonalities, the People Inside Us. John Rowan 1990[84]

What we call our *personality* is actually a collection of subpersonalities. Subpersonalities are a way of explaining how a one-dimensional person can have a multidimensional discussion with him- or herself. Years ago, one of the jokes about people was that it was OK to talk yourself—as long as you didn't answer. Answering implied that you were crazy. In reality, a dialogue (from the Greek and Latin root *duo, two, apart*) requires a minimum of two participants. Ask yourself, "Who am I talking to when I engage in self-talk?" There had to be somebody else in there I was talking to, someone who was responding to my queries or dictates or evaluating a course of action that I was proposing, right? Hence, another *subpersonality*. Perhaps a part of our personality who was questioning whether what we thought was a fact was the fact. Subpersonalities are not apparent as long as we are engaging in a behavior that is relatively automatic and consistent with the beliefs in that subpersonality. The subpersonality whose task it is to deal with this particular event is the part that's making the decisions. If we're disciplining a child for inappropriate behavior, there's typically not a question in our minds about how we ought to proceed. When we are attempting to solve a math problem, it's not an issue that requires any emotion or any permission to do anything. It's simply a matter of applying the tools we have to solve a problem.

Subpersonalities make an observable appearance when we have a dilemma. When we are in trouble, we may revert to behaviors that we used as children to avoid punishment—a little white lie, a coquettish smile, or some other strategy that helped us avoid punishment in the past. When it's time to comfort someone who's in distress, we have a list of appropriate behaviors in our repertoire to apply to the situation. *Understanding subpersonalities and acknowledging their existence allows us to examine what part of the personality allows us to hurt ourselves.*

When I ask my substance-abusing patients to pick up their pen or pencil and then stick themselves in the eye with it, they laugh. What an absurd request! None of them will deny that substance abuse is self-harm, yet they still engage in the behavior. The question arises, how can someone who knows full well that substance abuse is harmful leave treatment and begin hurting themselves again? While they are in treatment in a rehabilitation facility, while they have *voluntarily suspended substance abuse,* they readily admit that when someone else (the *executive of their personality,* their parent and/or adult ego state) is making the decision about what is appropriate or inappropriate behavior, they can control their own behavior. The reality is that substance abuse is a behavior under their control, not that of anyone else.

If it is true that self-harm is a choice, why do so many relapse? There are multiple reasons why relapse is so prevalent. Think back to the reinforcement schedules that control behavior. When a particular behavior has been committed hundreds, perhaps even thousands of times, the behavior is highest on the priority list for dealing with a range of situations. Typical for the addict, substance abuse is the go-to behavior for reducing the stress caused by any number of disappointments, threats to the ego, negative feelings, and so on. Many addicts have operated within the addiction subculture for so long that functioning in the normal society of non-abusers is uncomfortable and no longer part of their skill set. It is far simpler to continue relationships that are comfortable in the substance-abusing subculture. Felony criminal histories, fines, penalties, loss of license, loss of children, and loss of family support all come with long-term substance abuse. Reintegration is extremely difficult. If treatment did not address the underlying maladaptive schemas and self-destructive behavior patterns, then all rehab would produce is a dry drunk or addict.

Subpersonalities are observable and are grouped together by their role for our personality. After fifty years of looking at personality from this point of view, it is fairly well established that there are a minimum of six, possibly seven (with the subdivision of the parent ego state into positive and negative aspects), subpersonalities at play here. The subpersonalities are, in fact, observable *states of the ego.* This is where transactional analysis provides the cues by which we can know which personality (or part thereof) is responding to the situation with which we are confronted.

Subpersonalities and/or ego states are schemas. My beliefs and the contents of my ego states remain fixed until I find a reason to change them.

Transactional Analysis

Transactional Analysis was created by Dr. Eric Berne following a therapeutic exchange with one of his patients and presented in his book, *Games People Play* (Eric Berne, MD 1964)

A *transaction* is a unit of communication between individuals. It can be as simple as a gesture, a sigh, a glance, a touch, or a change in *posture or tone of voice, vocabulary,* or *facial expression.* These are the ways we can know which of the *ego states* or *subpersonalities* the other person communicating with us is using. These are observable behaviors that we all understand intuitively. Transactional analysis simply systematizes what we already know. For example, when people are angry with us, their voices are loud. They sound angry and act in a controlling fashion. They tell us what we should or shouldn't do. From these cues, we know that they're using the part of their personality that wants to tell people what to do and control things. This is called the *critical parent ego state.* If we adapt and do what we are told to do, the angry, controlling parental ego state will go away. If instead we decide that they don't have the right to tell us what to do or how to do it, then we will typically go to *our* parental ego state to let them know we have no intention of complying. This *crossed transaction* is how interactions escalate into second- and third-degree behavior that can result in tissue damage—the "My daddy's bigger than your daddy" syndrome.

Ego States

Talking to yourself doesn't mean *you are schizophrenic*; it means the different parts of your personality are discussing an issue and determining which part gets to make the decision about how to handle a situation or choose between alternatives.

Ego states are self-contained and complete sets of thoughts, feelings, beliefs, and behaviors. Transactional analysis identifies seven different ego states/subpersonalities that are definable by the functions that they perform for the personality. More recently, the critical and nurturing parental ego states have been subdivided into their positive and negative attributes. An ego state is a schema (as stated above), replete with a complete set of thoughts, facts, beliefs, feelings, and behaviors for dealing with an aspect of the environment. Each ego state has a repertoire for dealing with an aspect of the environment.

Transactional analysis was born in therapeutic encounters. Dr. Eric Berne was conducting a therapeutic interview when one of his patients asked whether he (Dr. Berne) wanted to talk to "the lawyer or the little boy." What appeared to be a strange request was, in fact, the birth of transactional analysis. Transactional analysis is not the same as Sigmund Freud's id, ego, and superego. Indeed, Freud's id and superego were not observable but only inferred.

Berne's transactional analysis focuses on behaviorally definable and observable "states of the ego," or ego states. Classic TA defines an ego state as a complete set of thoughts, feelings, and behaviors. TA posits that there are basically six ego states/subpersonalities that are pretty much grouped by their function. More recently there has been a move to redefine the parental ego states into healthy and unhealthy subparts. The *nurturing parent* is one of the ego states whose function it is to nurture and take care of ourselves and others; the nurturing parent has been divided into subcategories; a *realistic caregiver* and a *negative enabler*. The *critical* or *controlling parent* is the "rule giver," the part that bosses people around, telling them what is supposed to be done and how they are supposed to do it. This parental ego state has been subdivided into the *healthy rule giver* and the *tyrant rule giver*. The *adult* is tasked with *probability estimating and reality testing*. For substance abusers, it is the part that finally acknowledges that the thought processes and behaviors that allow them to continue to hurt themselves through substance abuse are not working.

The subpersonalities or ego states of the *child* are broken down as the parent in the child as one part of which is the *witch* or the *ogre* (depending on gender). This subpersonality observes how the parents or parent surrogates in its life controls the behavior of people around them. The adult in the child, affectionately known as the *little professor,* is the part of the personality that knows when it's time to be adaptive to avoid negative consequences (how to whine, cry, beg, and manipulate to get its way with all of its childlike wiles). While this may be very cute during the toddler stage, it's not as amusing as toddlers get older. It typically does not learn from experience and assumes that it can avoid consequences. When it is being adaptive, it is usually sufficiently frightened that it is over-adaptive and doesn't make rational decisions. The sixth ego state is the *free child*, the part of us that delights in just about everything around it. The following diagram depicts the structural analysis of our observable ego states.

Nurturing Parent

Critical Parent

Adult

Child

Rebellious

Adaptive
"Little Professor"

Free

These are the 6 "states of the ego", Ego States. They are observable and identifiable by attending to the 4 cues: Posture, Vocabulary, Tone of Voice and Expression /Demeanor. Each Ego State Has a "job". Critical Parent controls and dictates speaking in absolutes. Nurturing parent soothes and comforts. Adult asks questions, Who, What, Where, When Why etc. Rebellious Child talks back, Adapted Child does what it is told to and the Free child enjoys the world.

Typically, when I introduce these notions, I am met with curious looks. When I ask an individual or group if they talk to themselves, the answer is always yes. I then ask, "If there's just one personality inside us, who are you talking to?" Their own internal dialogue makes it possible to understand that the subpersonalities are carrying on a dialogue to decide which subpersonality will win the discussion and dictate what behaviors. For example when they are in the discomfort of withdrawal the internal dialogue is "go to detox and get clean" nurturing parent and adult versus "get more of the drug to avoid withdrawal" child, poor reality testing. They're trying to decide which will become the executive of the personality. Addicts who have been in rehab describe this interaction in the following way. An unpleasant event on the job, a relationship issue, financial or legal problems or loss of another sort creates emotional distress. In the past emotional distress was handled by postponing dealing with it by making it disappear chemically with their drug of choice, at least for a minute. Following rehab cognitive interventions have been acquired. One of them is to access the **adult ego state** and "play the tape out" of what happens if I use again, while another part, the **child ego state** opines you can use "just one more time and control it this time" to remove this bad feeling. We have a set of behaviors that are proscriptive for most situations. These are self-selected boundaries we set for those situations.

There are three basic types of transactions: they can be complementary, crossed, or duplex/ulterior.

Much like schemas, ego states are knowable and observable based on behavioral cues that are easily recognizable, even by young children. Children know which part (ego state) of the parental figures in their lives are currently interacting with them by the following observable cues: *posture, demeanor, tone of voice*, and *vocabulary*. The next diagram provides brief descriptions of the cues that we utilize to make an assessment of which ego state(s) the person or persons we are interacting with are in. The same cues allow us to know which ego state is making decisions that affect all of the ego states. In the case of addiction, it is a *harmful script* (from the Greek *hamartia*) that makes the decision to continue to hurt oneself. Scripts are life plans we decide on early in life. Much like early maladaptive schemas, they are incorporated from parental introjects, (statements that are intended to define one) who are in a position to tell us who we are, what our worth is, and what we're going to turn out to be. We divide the parent into two parts, the critical parent (who, in fits of impropriety, tells us the negative traits we possess) and the nurturing parent (who tells us good things about ourselves).

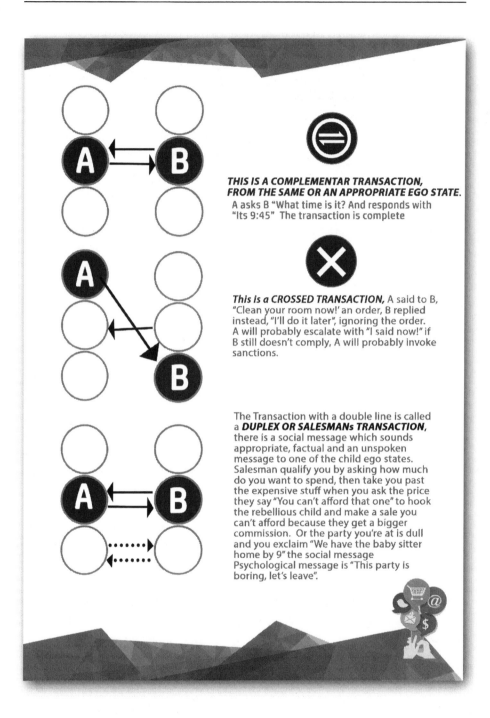

THIS IS A COMPLEMENTAR TRANSACTION, FROM THE SAME OR AN APPROPRIATE EGO STATE.
A asks B "What time is it? And responds with "Its 9:45" The transaction is complete

This is a CROSSED TRANSACTION, A said to B, "Clean your room now!' an order, B replied instead, "I'll do it later", ignoring the order. A will probably escalate with "I said now!" if B still doesn't comply, A will probably invoke sanctions.

The Transaction with a double line is called a **DUPLEX OR SALESMANs TRANSACTION,** there is a social message which sounds appropriate, factual and an unspoken message to one of the child ego states. Salesman qualify you by asking how much do you want to spend, then take you past the expensive stuff when you ask the price they say "You can't afford that one" to hook the rebellious child and make a sale you can't afford because they get a bigger commission. Or the party you're at is dull and you exclaim "We have the baby sitter home by 9" the social message Psychological message is "This party is boring, let's leave".

Programming the Human Biocomputer Revisited

Early human mental development is readdressed here with a more complete exploration of the work of Jean Piaget, on the formal operations acquisition in cognitive development; the work of Dr. Katherine Nelson, on the role of language in cognitive development; and the work of Dr. Lawrence Kohlberg, [85] on moral development. All three add volumes of data and lend credibility to the role of experience, nurture, and our understanding of the acquisition and expression of cognitive belief systems. Thorough treatment of the above would extend this work beyond the scope of addressing the need for a paradigm shift in the prevailing addiction schema.

The initial description of what a human being is born with in terms of information about itself—its *mind*—was limited and described as a *tabula rasa*, or blank slate. If it is accurate to assert that we are born with capacity but not specific information, how does a newborn *biocomputer* acquire information about who it is, what its worth is, and what it's going to be?

When we are young, we serve and survive at the pleasure of whoever guarantees our survival. Unfortunately, we do not require adults to pass a course on appropriate child-rearing techniques. There is no manual. It is assumed that if you are biologically capable of creating life (i.e., possess mature sex organs), you know how to shepherd a child into adequate adulthood. Nothing could be more inaccurate or further from the truth. Many of the addicts I deal with are children of substance-abusing parents, inappropriate role models, criminals, parents who are either incapable or unwilling to be affectionate or tell their children that they are loved, victims of inappropriate foster-care environments, or adoptees. Recall those who suffer from the ACEs; many are victims of abuse or neglect. Many were the targets of inadvertent negative self-concepts at the hands of their peers—arguably the most important sources of information regarding yourself once you leave the home environment to attend school. It is important to understand that the parents are not always to blame; a child may easily misconstrue the intent of parental messages and dictates.

Parents who don't understand that they are programming a new mind (the human biocomputer) can either purposely or inadvertently set their child on a self-destructive path. When they tell us we're dirty, nasty, or awful, and that we will never amount to anything or be worth anything, the effects can be profound. "Why do you always mess up?" and "Why can't you ever be right?" can be devastating to hear. Children are already programmed to believe that they can never do anything right, will never amount to anything, or are stupid, ugly, worthless, and more. This is the code to program a child for self-abuse. When we're abandoned, neglected, or abused sexually, physically, or mentally, we are programmed for self-abuse. Remember, the egocentricity of the developing mind assumes that *whatever happens to me was caused by me.* Parents inadvertently reinforce this belief by telling children, "I didn't want to spank you, *but you made me do it!*" (I do recall that I sometimes preferred a spanking to a litany of my defects.)

The information that the child is receiving from caregivers and others in her/his environment forms the core elements of what we describe as a self-concept. "Rather, the claim here is that language opens up possibilities for sharing and retaining memories for both personal and social functions. Among the most important of these functions is the establishment of a self-history that serves as a source for self-understanding and an enduring self-concept."[86]

We know that our personal language, which is the way we eventually represent ourselves in the world, becomes our fact rather than a concept offered by somebody else. Why, as posited before, do we not have the cognitive or intellectual skills to dispute or refute the information regarding our self? We know from research that there are "voices in the mind," which are memories of dialogue we have heard in the past.

Those of you who have or have been around toddlers are probably painfully aware of the fact that they incorporate dialogue they overhear from those around them and repeat it at the most inopportune times. "Where did you here that word, OOPS?" Children seem to be exceptionally open to a variety of different voices and are able to 're-invoice' them quite accurately from early development. This 'concept of self' becomes incorporated in our internal vernacular and is our self-definition."[87] This is another validation of the role of self-talk in the creation of what we believe about ourselves. This definition/description of what we think and feel about our self will place us squarely in one of the quadrants of the OK Corral as well.

Another one of the pragmatic absolutes of transactional analysis lends its title to the next section.

Reality Testing Is a Function of a Discrete Adult Ego State

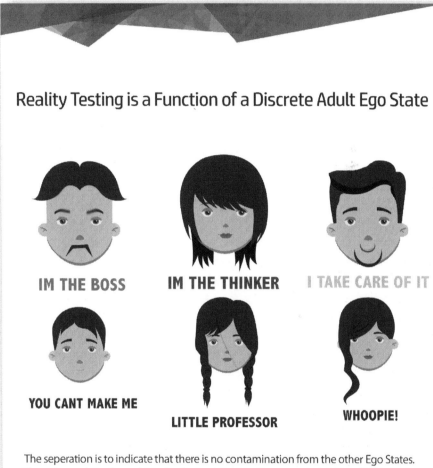

Reality Testing is a Function of a Discrete Adult Ego State

IM THE BOSS   IM THE THINKER   I TAKE CARE OF IT

YOU CANT MAKE ME

LITTLE PROFESSOR

WHOOPIE!

The seperation is to indicate that there is no contamination from the other Ego States. There is no data thought to be factual that isn't supported with reliable Data.

DISCRETE ADULT EGO STATE

Addicts will tell you that their relapse was caused by thinking and truly believing that they could use one more time and control it, despite the fact that they had tried it before and it didn't work. *I burnt my hand on the hot stove, but this time the hot stove won't burn.* The word *discrete* in the pragmatic absolute regarding reality testing is stating clearly that the adult ego state was not contaminated by either the child or parent ego states. Why? When you have relapsed even once with that inaccurate representation of your own adult thinking, it should be patently obvious that the next round of that behavior will end with the same result—re-addiction. Einstein defined insanity well as: "Doing the same thing over again and expecting a different result," This is what *No Reality Testing looks like, ignoring data that has already been tested and confirmed.*. When addicts get honest during treatment, they freely admit that it is not the adult ego state that allows them to use.

It is the ability to discriminate between ego states and understand the contamination that allows addicts to understand both why and how they have ignored the information in their adult lives that could have kept them from continuing the maladaptive behavior. For those of you who are not addicted to illicit substances, ask yourself why you smoke, overeat, gamble, or engage in any behavior that you know is not in your best interest.

Think back to Dr. Berne's patient who asked if he wanted to talk to the lawyer or the little boy; once these concepts have been explained and acknowledged, many patients discuss their maladaptive behavior as if it were developed sometime during childhood. They recognize it is the child ego state that makes the decision now to abuse substances or continue other maladaptive behaviors. It is not uncommon for them to blame the eight-year-old who is controlling their personality at that time. They understand that it is some other part of the personality that invades the adult (contamination of the adult) and initiates the self-destructive behavior. It can be the child ego state that says, "I won't get caught" or "I can control it—this time"; the critical parent that punishes for some transgression, real or imagined; or the nurturing parent that takes pity on the child and says, "Go ahead and use; I know you're dope sick and hurting."

The reality is that addicts are not stupid; they know what they're doing, they know what the consequences of substance abuse are—and yet, they do it anyway. There is not one among us who does not have the capability of justifying any behavior that we want to engage in. To violate social or ethical norms requires a malformed or missing (excluded) parent, a misinformed adult, or a rebellious child. The majority of these conditions are the result of actions, inactions, or misconceptions of the environment that children were raised in, and the result is the development of maladaptive schemas. Maladaptive schemas can develop as the unintended consequences of *the inability of children to accurately construe the intentions of their caregivers.*

Contamination and Exclusion

Contamination occurs when you think the response is coming from one ego state and it's actually coming from another ego state. Those who have used to the point of addiction, cleaned up and then relapsed more than once thinking they could now drink responsibly already have that data/fact in their adult, that the odds are slim at best, yet try it again. In reality the adapted child, the "little professor" is actually making the decision but saying "I can handle it now".

Exclusion occurs when one or more ego states are excluded from any decision making process for reasons that make sense to the part doing the excluding. "Dry drunks" are typically unhappy and have excluded the child ego state for fear that if they allow any part of the child to participate in decision making, like have fun, they will lose control and relapse. Others are uncomfortable expressing feelings for fear of being vulnerable. Addicts in full addiction exclude or ignore the adult who knows that the next injection could lead to an overdose and death, or the next drink could produce a blackout and place them in harm's way, or smoke when they have COPD.

CONTAMINATION

The child ego state has contaminated the adult by convincing it that it can now control the intake of their drug of choice.

EXCLUSION

The child of the addict has excluded both the parent and the adult to avoid recognizing the consequences of addiction, they are ignored.

Shifts between ego states take only a nanosecond. We (the *adult*) can be having a congenial conversation with a friend, colleague, or family member, discussing one of the taboo topics—politics or religion—and make a statement construed as "goring" one of the other person's "sacred cows," like suggesting that Rush Limbaugh, Bill O'Reilly, or Chris Matthews are puppets of their political-party affiliation and distort facts to support their attacks against the opposing political party. It could also be a comment from an Evangelical Christian who states that Catholicism is a cult, or the current battle over what to call ISSL between the "hawks and doves." Immediately, the person whose "ox got gored" goes on the offensive or defensive, and the conversation is no longer congenial.

These beliefs are schemas and are just as resistant to change as the EMSs of addictions. Have you ever tried to convince a friend to change his or her political affiliation? Good luck! Once a schema is formed, we want to keep it, regardless of any contradictory data presented regarding its validity. We are still arguing over the contribution of fossil-fuel burning to the greenhouse effect—as the polar ice caps melt, glaciers recede, oceans rise, and mean temperatures increase. The facts are indisputable, but if you have a reason to want to continue burning fossil fuels, you dispute the facts because they disagree with your schema or would limit your personal gain, another schema. Personal gain, namely the accumulation of wealth, is more important than the health of the planet.

Scripts, Survival Strategies, TA Games, Character Defects, Injunctions, and Counter injunctions

Schemas are our internalized belief systems regarding how our lives are going to be. As such, they become *survival strategies*. That means it is our belief that these strategies, these belief systems, are necessary for our survival. Survival strategies are at the core of our belief systems regarding how we must behave in order to survive. As such, they are extremely resistant to change. In TA terms, they become *scripts*. Scripts are road maps for our lives; they are life plans, no different than a script in a play or a screenplay. All the elements are there—heroes, villains, plot twists, a beginning, the middle, and an end. All of the characters necessary to complete our life plan we manage to find or create. If my lot in life is to be the victim of an abusing man or woman, people who have this script tell me they can walk into any bar or any other situation and pick out the person who will fulfill this expectation. There are three basic script types: winners, hamartic (from the Greek for *harmful*), and banal. Obviously, this trichotomy represents and encompasses continuums.

Addiction scripts are like Greek tragedies; they always end with the demise of the main character. When I ask the resident populations whether they know who Icarus and Sisyphus are and describe their stories, they recognize the same repetitious self-defeating behavior in themselves.. The majority of the addicts I've dealt with began altering their reality with psychotropics early on, typically in their teens or preteens, and now (in their twenties, thirties, forties, and fifties) don't see a way out of their addiction. A tragic end is their prediction if they don't succeed in this last-ditch attempt at rehabilitation. Most of them have already overdosed (OD'd) at least once, blacked out numerous times, observed friends OD, and accumulated legal sanctions, misdemeanors, felonies, and DUIs. Many have served time in jail and prison, and yet they continue to engage in the behaviors that result in these outcomes. The full-length version of the script issues can be found in C. Steiner's *Scripts People Live*.[88]

Scripts are generated by positive and negative parental injunctions. Injunctions are immutable dictates, mandates, and truths. They are what your caregivers and other significant individuals in your environment used to describe you to you. Who would know better than the person who holds your survival in their grasp? They describe you to you in the following ways; "You will never amount to anything." "You are a loser, just like your (pick a parent)." "You are evil/have a mean streak/ have a bad temper." "Girls don't understand math." This was one of my own personal injunctions: "You will be in jail before you are twenty-one." OK, I complied; I spent three days in the drunk tank, and I had to put *minor in possession of alcohol* on any job application for years. Is there any doubt that addiction would facilitate the actualization of these harmful scripts?

Negative injunctions are the "don'ts": don't be (live), don't feel, don't think, don't succeed, don't be healthy, don't be happy, and so on, that create self-destructive scripts. Many addicts create very successful businesses only to destroy them, regain sobriety, and build another one, only to destroy it again. The pattern of succeeding and then self-sabotaging is the hallmark of a hamartic (harmful) script. It is the repetition of the negative outcome pattern over time that allows for the designation of the behavior as script driven. It always ends the same way, though there are always minor deviations: "I had ninety days clean," or "I was sober for three years," and so on.

Counter injunctions are the positive "dos." They are the antithesis of the negative injunctions. All of the positives: be happy, healthy, successful, smart, intelligent, gentle, kind, a great parent, and so on. One study indicated that alcoholics were significantly higher than nonalcoholic controls on three positive injunctions: *please others, be perfect*, and *try hard*.[89] What happens to you when you can't fulfill these injunctions? Unfortunately, if the parent is actually mentally ill or a severe anti-social personality disorder, they can unintentionally direct you on a self-destructive path: "It's OK for you to use psychotropics, smoke, drink, and do drugs as long as you do it at home." It's more important for the parent to be your friend than your parent. The fly in the ointment is which script/counter script did your environment support? We have now come full circle; we are back to how many ACEs you were exposed to.

What maladaptive schemas did you develop? The harmful script can find some remedial relief in the counter injunctions to the script, but the inevitable return is to the harmful script. It is a life plan; untreated it is doomed to repeat. History unexamined is doomed to repeat itself.

Games are a series of transactions we have learned to play that will result in the emotional response we expect, actually require, in transactions with other people that will give us the outcome or feeling we believe we have coming. If we don't feel good about ourselves, one of the ways to prop up our self-esteem is by helping others, whether they need it or not. The name of the game is ITHY—as in, "I'm only trying to help you!" In this game, we do things for people without asking them if they want us to. By this process, we get to feel good about ourselves while at the same time discounting the other person's ability to do something for him- or herself. These are the people we define as rescuers: individuals who discount someone else's ability to think or do for themselves.

One of the favorite games of addicts and others who are leading unproductive lives is the "Wooden Leg" game. In this game, the person who is engaging in self-destructive behavior tells you that he or she is not doing better because his or her addiction is biological—and what do you expect from a guy/gal with a "wooden leg" (a biological disorder beyond his conscious control)? This answer divests the person of all responsibility for his or her behavior. People who feel bad about themselves like to play a game called "Kick Me." They find someone who needs to feel superior, who will remind them of some defect they have, so that they can feel bad about themselves and the other player can feel superior. Games are fascinating. There are multiple websites that describe the seven steps of games resulting in an emotional payoff that validates one's life position. Put *TA Games* in the search bar and enjoy. For a full description of games, see Eric Berne's *Games People Play*.

Character defects are the way that AA and NA describe and address *games people play*, by having individuals in recovery examine the way they use words, feeling states, and behaviors to manipulate and control the environment they choose to live in. The expectation in AA and NA is that you will examine and begin to understand how you use words, feelings, behaviors, and concepts to manipulate your way through life.

The constant high rate of relapse among addicts maintains and supports the belief that it is a biological disorder or disease. The belief that you won't change until you really "reach your bottom" is blaming the addict's biology for being unchangeable, and the justification of failed treatment. How then does actually reaching your bottom alter your biology? It sounds more like an acknowledgment (*a cognitive decision*) that, "I don't want this anymore, and I don't have the knowledge to fix it." It is the realization that I have finally reached this stage in my recovery where I recognize the following for the third time: I no longer discount that *I have a problem*. I no longer discount that *the problem is serious*. I acknowledge and recognize that *the problem is solvable*. I recognize that I do *have the ability to solve it*.

These are *cognitive* (not biological) reactions, conclusions, and decisions. There is an actual change in the addict's mental state, in which all the tricks and cognitive distortions are finally abandoned in hopes of actually achieving recovery. The difficulty arises when the addict, after obtaining a period of sobriety, must reenter the parts of society that he or she may have avoided for years. Many of the addicts I deal with have only marginally participated in the nondrug culture for up to twenty or thirty years; the adolescents, who have been immersed in the drug subculture for ten years, must now assimilate when they don't have any friends who are sober and their families have abandoned them. What they report is boredom and negative feelings; not having any sober friends leaves them feeling incredibly lonely.

Since we are herd animals, this alienation makes using again a viable option. One of the real pluses of AA and NA is that it does provide a community of individuals who are attempting to maintain their sobriety through the fellowship of others who are doing the same. One of the metaphors that AA uses is this: "If an alcoholic car thief obtains sobriety, what do you call him/her? A sober car thief." By not completing the hard work of understanding why you have been hurting yourself, you remain in the same position—a sober person with the self-defeating belief systems that guide your harmful script.[90] This is an indictment of some AA/NA sponsors who have no idea how, why, or what the people they are providing treatment to have been exposed to.

Successful psychotherapeutic intervention relies on three principles. *Potency* is the belief that the person you trust with the awesome task of changing the way you view yourself knows what he or she is doing and possesses the knowledge and training to guide you through the resolution of the presenting problem. Do you have a comorbid disorder, does your sponsor know what one is and the appropriate treat-ment strategy is for one? In the AA/NA community, that means someone who has obtained a certain level of sobriety by completing the 12 steps. Unfortunately, your treatment is left to the individual sponsor's discretion. I know of rehab graduates with less than a year of sobriety under their belts who offer themselves as sponsors to in-dividuals new to their sobriety. *Protection* is the reassurance that your confidentiality will be maintained. The treating professional is required to present you with a manda-tory disclosure document listing their skill-set and treat only what they are skilled in. They will inform you who to contact if they violate the conditions of the relationship with inappropriate behavior. *Permission: as nonsensical as this sounds permission from the therapist* is needed to change the self-destructive thinking and behaviors that keep you ill

CHAPTER 7

Summary: The Paradigm Shift

ACEs ▶ EMSs ▶ *Mental Disorders* ▶ *Self-Medication* ▶ *Addiction*

W hat I find most egregious is the fact that the work of Felliti and Anda on the effects of ACEs on addiction has been around for almost twenty years but has made no impact on the existing paradigm. Twenty years multiplied by 500,000+ deaths per annum equals ten million possibly avoidable deaths.

When I began this quest, I thought I was among a small minority of clinicians and other interested parties who were struck by the apparent anomalies in my observations of what I thought was a random sample of the SUD population. Sifting through the data, a pattern began to emerge. There were lines of research from diverse fields, dismembering the long-held belief that addiction was a biological disease. They were finding that it is probably not a chronically relapsing brain disease marked by compulsive drug seeking. Did the population definitely exhibit self-destructive behavior? Yes. Did the research support the disease model? No. Was there a more viable explanation moving the addiction needle out of the "incurable" category? Yes.

Imagine my delight when I read the NIAAA article called "Alcoholism Isn't What It Used to Be." They weren't redefining its status as a disease, but they were acknowledging that one could drink excessively without becoming an alcoholic—with no automatic hijacking and compulsive drug seeking. When Dr. Willenbring described how the population of drinkers may actually be two populations, intermittent/chronic and time-limited, it permitted alternative explanations to be entertained. He also acknowledged that they "had painted with too broad a brush" in building their model of addiction based on the intermittent/chronic because they were the ones who had presented for treatment; that mistake skewed the data.

By, acknowledging that most substance abusers quit on their own the door for the alternative explanation that what we see clinically may actually be outliers, or those not representative of the population it was assumed they represented. These findings created the opportunity to consider a more definitive explanation of this *aberrant, self-destructive behavior*. The data presented from a variety of sources—physiological, psychological, epistemological, social, philosophical, foreign, and epidemiological sources—provides a more compelling argument for a *thinking disorder* versus the "hijacked brain," compulsive drug seeking, and a chronically relapsing brain (physiological) disease, which completely ignores the frontal and prefrontal cortices of the human cognitive apparatus.

An alternate explanation is based on the relationship between comorbid mental disorders and SUDs. Data was presented on the high rates of co-occurrence between *DSM-5* mental disorders and SUDs by those who met the *clinical criteria* for inclusion. That means it is an underestimate, because those with *subclinical symptoms* were excluded from the cohort. The usual comorbid disorders were presented to validate the suspected antecedent environmental conditions precipitating the mental disorder. Part and parcel of those descriptions are the references to the types of trauma that produce mental disorders. Adverse childhood events (ACEs) are specific types of trauma precipitating different mental disorders. These adverse traumatic environments create schemas about one's place in the world that are maladaptive, produce life plans (scripts) that are harmful, and reinforce neural pathways through repeated reinforcement of inappropriate behavior. These maladaptive schemas lead to a variety of behaviors that are disruptive to the normal development of the frontal and prefrontal cortices, which are still developing through adolescence into early adulthood.

Treatment needs to focus on the traumas that set self-destructive behavior into motion. Once inertia is overcome, a body set in motion will remain in motion.

When I began this book, I thought I was in a minority with my belief system regarding addiction. I was not as alone as I thought. I am adding my voice to those who have been data driven and also find the existing paradigm not only lacking but dangerous to those in need of service. To rely on outdated beliefs that remain unsupported by facts and not offer best-practice treatment strategies is inconsistent with the mandate to *first, do no harm*.

Addiction is a thinking disorder, best treated by examining the inaccuracies in one's self-perception created by ACEs perpetrated on children by uninformed, unaware, or disturbed persons or environments on the susceptibility of children to environmental input. Trauma-based treatment works. We have successfully employed this treatment strategy for the last seventeen years at the Stout Street Foundation.

CHAPTER 8

The Nonsecular Approach to Addiction Treatment

Celebrate Recovery

I have not been able to find any systematic assessment of the efficacy of this approach. The group was founded in 1990 by Pastor John Baker[91] of the Saddleback Church. Celebrate Recovery was started because its founders did not believe that the existing AA reliance on an undefined higher power was sufficiently definitive or should be explicitly defined as God. They have bolstered the twelve steps with biblical references for each one. They advertise that their approach treats "hurts, habits, and hang ups," including substance and sexual abuse. The small sample of anecdotal information I have received from members who left stated that they left because the type of information they were seeking was not available with this approach. The model as they understood it did not allow others in the group to provide strategies for problem solving.

AA/NA

The predominant model (I use the term *model* as it's not a scientific fact) regarding addiction is the AA model, adopted by NA as well. It is accepted by the general, religious, legal, scientific, and medical communities as the preferred treatment option for addiction in its various forms (e.g., eating, gambling, and sex addictions). It is estimated that a vast 70–80 percent of all treatment facilities rely on or utilize the AA model in some capacity.[13]

Regardless of the addiction, the basic premise remains the same: the way to control (not cure) it is to acknowledge the addiction; acknowledge your powerlessness over the "disease"; rely on the of your higher power to help you control what you haven't been able to; define yourself as defective so you won't forget; obtain a sponsor (an individual who has demonstrated control over his or her own addiction); and join a support community you can turn to when temptation rears its ugly head (which it surely will).

Implicit in the name of the organizations, *anonymous* is the mandate to maintain the anonymity of the membership. It is understandable that despite the acceptance of the disease model (which absolves addicts of personal responsibility for their actions), anonymity is helpful. Unfortunately, the "disease" is still viewed with the taint of a moral failing by most of the public. This term, *anonymous*, makes validation of their claims (that if you faithfully follow the program, you will remain clean and sober) unavailable for scientific scrutiny.

This is not a blanket indictment of AA/NA; if you rigidly follow the program, you can remain clean and sober. There are hundreds of thousands (perhaps millions) who have remained sober after submitting to the AA/NA programs. The unfortunate part, which is not addressed, is the success rate of AA. It is perfect for those who follow it religiously. However, it appears that only about 5–8 percent of those who try AA are successful, and that's only if they remain in the AA community after a year; 40–60 percent drop out in the first year.[47]

The obvious question to me—as a scientist and treating professional—is, how did the *other* 92–95 percent fare? The SHARP Study found that those treated by AA, when compared to three different cognitive behavioral treatment options and a no-treatment control group, demonstrated a significant increase in binge drinking. The authors concluded that no treatment might be a viable option. In the study conducted by Brandsma et al. in 1980, the population consisted of 260 individuals: 184 were court referred and 76 were either self-referred or referred by other agencies. The groups were followed for 210 days. Participants were randomly assigned to five different groups: a group who had to attend AA meetings run by experienced professionals; a group who had to have RBT administered by a nonprofessional; a group who had to have RBT administered by degreed professionals; a group who had to have insight therapy administered by professionals; and a control group who received no treatment. The study occurred almost forty years ago and admittedly possessed methodological flaws. All groups outperformed the control group.

Spirituality

God don't make no junk is a phrase I come across constantly in the recovery community. I phrase my inculcation on transactional analysis a little differently: "We were all born princes and princesses, and the events around us conspired to turn us into frogs." Incorporated in both of those descriptions are the innocence of children; none of us were born bad. Recall for a moment Maia Szalavitz's certain knowledge that she somehow knew she was inherently bad at five years of age.

My experience at the Salvation Army's City of Hope in Sarasota, Florida, added to my understanding of the necessity of spirituality in the recovery from addiction, especially for those who are outliers. In each of us there is an existential sense of who and what we are in the universe, the belief that we lay somewhere on the continuum of good and bad. It is fairly difficult to live in a world where there is a Tao for everything. We typically insist that implicit in positing the existence of good is positing the existence of bad. We define white as the absence of color and black as a composite of all colors. As much as I dislike absolutes, I will state that the outlier addict population define themselves in the most odious of ways: definitely bad. They view their behavior as reprehensible and unforgivable, despite a forgiving God. The existence of ACEs and the creation of EMSs from neglect and abuse create a lack of self-worth that is played out through self-destructive behavior. They have always known they were damaged goods and acted in ways that proved the validity of that conclusion.

Build a Bridge and Get Over It!

Let me begin my praise of AA/NA by acknowledging the tools they added to my toolbox of treatment strategies. I have always recognized the massive amount of guilt and self-loathing that addicts carry when they stop using long enough to examine their behavior. The fourth AA step attempts to address these behaviors by having them examine what acts/deeds they committed for which they need to make amends. In the past I always referred my patients to someone with "moral authority" (someone who shares the spiritual beliefs of their choice) when I did not believe I had the moral authority or credentials to adequately deal with their spiritual beliefs. I couldn't hear the confessions of a Catholic because I'm not a priest and could not mete out the appropriate sanctions leading to absolution. In the past, I essentially provided only lip service: "Go see the spiritual advisor of your choice for these moral dilemmas." I now recognize that exploring these areas is critical to recovery.

What I found is that many are unable to forgive themselves, as they believe their transgressions are unforgivable. They are unable to separate the person from the behavior: "I am what I did." I would urge all clinicians to incorporate an assessment of our patients' stances on these issues. How does a person stop self-destructive behavior when his or her transgressions are unforgivable? Self-hate and loathing, and an unforgiving view of same, are impediments to recovery. All of you who have treated victims of early sexual, physical, and emotional abuse know that a key element in recovery is removing the belief that they had in some way *caused* the abuse.

AA/NA are helping thousands, perhaps millions, of people. I'm certain that many in AA will find it arrogant of me to question or appear to criticize AA and NA in any way. After all, they're "only trying to help." In the helping business, it's important to remember to "first, do no harm." I'm simply not certain that those of you who provide sponsorship have a full set of tools at your disposal to diagnose and treat a disorder that kills, destroys families, models inappropriate and self-destructive behaviors for children, robs our economy of billions of dollars, sends people to jail for nonviolent offenses, robs youth of socialization during critically important developmental years, and more. AA/NA have a questionable (possibly very low) success rate. I am not suggesting that you stop; I am asking that you take a close look at your success rate and ask yourself one question: "Am I doing no harm?" Is it possible that there are additions to your skill set that could increase the likelihood that you will be more successful with those who place their faith in you to alter their life course? Rather than be strident in your belief that "there's a right way, a wrong way, and the AA way," in what ways can you enhance your ability to help?

One of the major reasons AA/NA fail with the outliers is the belief that building a bridge and getting over it will solve the problem that created the need to anesthetize oneself. They are admonished by their sponsor or group "Be a man/woman and man up!" In other words, you are a whiny baby who just needs to get tough. Don't solve the underlying problem; ignore it!

Perhaps one of the major reasons why the AA/NA success rate is so low is because they do not screen for comorbid disorders like anxiety, depression, PTSD, and personality disorders. On the other hand, even if they did, do you think these disorders are unrelated or independent of the substance abuse (as opposed to the premise that what you call addiction may actually be *self-medication* for those disorders)? Are you aware that SUDs and comorbid disorders respond best to CBT? Do you use CBT or even know what it is?

I believe we all want the same thing and are all working toward the same goal: to teach those who are self-destructive to stop hurting themselves. We must pool our knowledge and resources and give up futile turf wars in support of archaic belief systems.

Sponsors, whether you recognize it or not, you are providing psychotherapy without a license. Your basic assumption—that addiction is a biological disorder—implies that your current strategy, a twelve-step treatment, could "do no harm." How can words do additional damage to a brain that's genetically disordered? Some of you have acquired the skill to deal with underlying disorders successfully. Dealing with psychiatric disorders isn't the exclusive domain of graduate school training programs. However, if you have not had specific training in the treatment of mental disorders, I would ask you the same question as I would ask any trained professional participating in the amelioration of a substance use disorder, "What is your success rate?"

Many of you in AA would reply, "It's progress, not perfection!" This is the classic response to the chronically relapsing brain-disease model. If you accept credit for your sponsee's recovery, are you also willing to accept responsibility for their failure? In the AA/NA communities, psychotherapy is meted out by *sponsors*. Many of these sponsors recognize that they don't have the knowledge or therapeutic skills to adequately treat some of the more severe types of trauma their *sponsee* has been exposed to. They recognize the limitations of their skills and refer their sponsee to persons who are trained to deal with specific traumas. When treating severe trauma, a common strategy of some sponsors is to encourage the sponsee they are working with to build a bridge and get over it. Some *sponsors* see suppression, repression, acceptance, rationalization, and denial as viable treatment options for early trauma. Their lack of awareness of the effects of severe abuse, neglect, and abandonment can produce a "dry drunk," who is sober—but miserable.

We define light as something that would not exist without dark. Unfortunately, by defining addiction to legal or illegal substances as bad, we create in addicts a sense that they, *as opposed to their behaviors*, have become bad. Bad is obviously the opposite of good. Addicts do not understand that there was an underlying malaise that prompted their reliance on addictive substances in the first place; hence, the need for *self-medication*. As a result, they take full responsibility with accompanying recriminations for their addictive behavior and the havoc it creates in the lives of those around them. They don't know where it came from or how they got it; they only know that they are bad people. Not that their *behavior* is bad, but that *they* are bad, defective-to-the-core people who are unwilling and unable to combat their "disease."

There is some comfort in believing that addiction is not a failure to act appropriately but instead an uncontrollable response that is produced by the "disease" in your brain. When I ask them how they voluntarily made their disease cease and desist, they reply with, "The environment does it." That is, the involuntary control that the disease produces responds to an environment where someone outside of them decides what appropriate and inappropriate behavior is. In TA terms, they have turned over the executive of their personality (the *adult*) to an outside source—the staff of the facility. Would it be useful to you as a sponsor to confront your sponsee with the information that their *mind* must do the next right thing in order to avoid relapse? Yes, relapses *can be* a part of recovery, *but not a required part*. Relapse occurs when the executive of the personality (the *adult*) abdicates its responsibility and allows the *child* in him or her to make the decision—"I can do it one more time and not get addicted again"—which every one of them knows is BS.

Barring unlimited resources, the process of being an addict is very expensive and, by necessity, has adverse consequences on the world we live in. If one has unlimited resources to purchase the substance of choice, that person is not required to violate the welfare of others. For those without unlimited resources for drugs (that are actually quite inexpensive to produce), once addiction has become a part of their life, they must now find ways to support their habit. Typically, this requires the violation of legal and social norms and personal moral predilections. In order to avoid withdrawal, the world around addicts is subject to the many nefarious ways they must behave in order to have a continual supply of their substances of choice. Typically, the easiest group to prey on is their immediate family. Now they are no longer just an *addict*; they have added another bad adjective to their description of self: *thief*.

When the family is no longer willing to turn the other cheek, providing an alternate source of income becomes imperative. Drug addiction is an expensive proposition, and previous definitions of self must now be given up in order to ward off the dragon of withdrawal. Almost any illegal act is an acceptable way to avoid withdrawal. Men and women alike become commercial sex workers and must add *whore, prostitute*, or *sexual deviant* to their descriptions of self. Some turn to manufacturing, selling, distributing, and luring others into their distribution system. These are but a few of the ways addicts support a habit. What do you think of a man or woman who describes him- or herself as a crack whore? The term is typically used to define females, but many men have assured me that "chicken queens" (older men who seek to have sex with young men) pay extremely well. *Faggot* and *queer* are extremely pejorative terms used by straight males even now, despite our recognition of alternative hypotheses, gender dysmorphic disorders, epigenetics, XXXY genetic codes, and more.

Those who have engaged in that type of fundraising to support their addiction have an extreme aversion to sharing that information. Sexual exploitation of women is age-old and recognized. Women who have chosen that strategy to support their habit are far more willing to share that information because it is more acceptable than male prostitution, something that is viewed as "an abomination before God." Women are more willing to share that they were sexually abused. Men who have been sexually abused are far less willing to admit to the abuse and are more likely to think they might be homosexual to explain their abuse. We seem to understand that women will be abused, but our homophobia implies that we must hide male-on-male abuse. Why? There will be rejection of this new awareness from many communities. We define sexual deviation from preexisting moral codes (see Kohlberg) as far more disgusting than other violations of social mores.

The point is, if they are unable to accept forgiveness, they leave the facility in a life position with the belief that they are still not acceptable to the culture at large. You are OK, and I am not OK, so I want to "get away from" you. How do you assimilate into a general culture that still perceives you (in your mind) to be unworthy? If you cannot assimilate into the non-addicted culture, then the options are some form of withdrawal or a return to the addictive subculture, where you will be accepted with open arms.

This caveat is intended for all who are involved in the field of addiction. Many treatment providers do not accept spirituality as any part of the domain in which they should be participating. When it is understood that forgiving the self is integral to continued sobriety, it becomes imperative that we address it as part of our treatment protocol. When funders look at a program and whether to support it financially, the fact that it has a spiritual component should not be a criterion for rejection. Those who train therapists at the lay, mid, or professional level will, I hope, recognize that our treatment must be multifaceted and that the self-perception of our patients is critical to success following treatment. Participating in an environment that accepts you with open arms increases the likelihood that you will begin to love yourself. The concept of loving yourself implies that you would not intentionally hurt someone you love, and participating in addiction is self-destructive behavior.

I hope I have piqued your interest to take a look at your addiction schema. There are many ways to know something. There is faith, science, and anecdotal information ("I heard about it" or "saw a case of it"). The scientific community must prove its assertions about a particular event by adhering to rules about how information (data) is collected, analyzed, and reported. Their assertions must be evaluated by their scientific peers before the data is incorporated into the scientific belief system as a fact. Even then, a "fact" is only a fact until some other scientist demonstrates that the observations were incomplete or flawed in some way. Other scientists must be able to replicate the results, or the data is suspect. (As illustration, I refer you to the current debate over global warming.)

The numerous attempts to empirically evaluate the effectiveness of AA/NA have produced mixed results, but the NIAAA acknowledgment that the population we have used to establish etiology was predicated on the behavior of outliers was inaccurate (my description, not theirs).

CHAPTER 9

Psychopathology, Psychopharmacology, Psychiatry, and the Biological Model (Nature vs. Nurture) Re-Re-Revisited Again

T here are several purposes for addressing the elaborate set of prescription drugs that become drugs of abuse. The first is to validate the premise that the drugs of abuse are consumed to alter the way addicts feel. So with each substance that is reviewed, it is important to understand what the effects are and with increased use, what the side effects are. The second is to inform the uninitiated that those prescription drugs that are relatively inexpensive when purchased legally have their value multiplied when they're sold illegally: Oxycodone, OxyContin, and Dilaudid can go for as much as $20 a pill on the streets, yet cost only a couple of dollars each legally. A ninety-day prescription, when taken three times a day, yields 270 pills. When sold at $20 each, that becomes $5,240. That's not bad for a few days' work, and this is how many addicts support their own habits. The drugs that are listed below are found in most medicine cabinets. Addicts, alcoholics, and adolescents are all aware of their value and are more than willing to remove them from your cabinet for their own use or to sell.

When we consult a psychiatrist, we are seeking relief for some mental discomfort, including anxiety, depression, a psychotic process (delusions, hallucinations, etc.), or emotional discomfort. They may offer a combination of psychotherapy and pharmaceutical relief from the troubling mental process, but more than likely, they stop at writing the script with the admonition to return in any number of days for review and evaluation. More often than not, a pharmaceutical solution is only offered based on the biological-model belief that a genetic disorder is causing a chemical imbalance. The purpose of breaking the chemical imbalance belief apart is to highlight the fact that we are specifically looking at the effects of various chemical compounds on the brain. What should be abundantly clear at this juncture is that *psychotropics* are taken because they *alter the mind, the way we feel*. It is this alteration in the way we feel that provides licit and illicit drugs with their *raison d'etre*—their purpose for being. We drink water to quench our thirst. We consume food to quench our hunger. We consume nicotine, alcohol, and legal and illicit drugs *to alter the way we feel*. Many of the drugs we take are designed to reduce or remove pain. A *secondary effect* of these drugs is that they also *alter the way we feel*, meaning they are *psychoactive*. When the pain from the original injury is no longer there, why would the painkiller continue to be consumed unless it had another positively reinforcing effect? The biological model posits that the brain, *not the mind*, has been *chemically hijacked* and the result is addiction. When addicts go cold turkey and stop using their drugs of choice, how do they "unhijack" the brain? Acts of volition are decisions of the mind, not the brain. They may be prompted by the discomfort of withdrawal to use, but it is the *mind* that decides to avoid the discomfort of withdrawal by using another mind-altering substance. When they reach the stage of desperation, they are willing to go to detox and work through the discomfort. Those addicts who have sufficient resources or are at risk for severe, life-threatening consequences can receive medical detox.

The side effect of almost all drugs that are consumed addictively is that they alter feelings and emotions. This fact is not my epiphany; this is information received directly from those who consume these substances addictively. Justifications are just that, even though they may discuss the effects of their drug of choice in laudatory terms such as these:

- "It's fun."
- "I like getting high."
- "It makes sex better."
- "I'm not as shy."
- "I have confidence."
- "I'm not uncomfortable in a group."
- "It keeps me from getting bored."

The reality is that once consumption has reached addictive levels, the positive side effects disappear. Addiction ensues when a drug is consumed in increasing quantities because habituation has occurred, and the drug is consumed in increasing quantities to avoid withdrawal. In the parlance of addiction, this is known as "getting dope sick" or "experiencing the DTs." Every day becomes a matter of, "How do I get my substance of choice? If I can't get it, what can I take to replace it?" Many addicts who altered feelings with opiates like Dilaudid and Oxycodone switch to heroin because it is cheaper and lasts longer. Crack is given up for methamphetamine, a cheaper and longer-lasting alternative. Heroin is currently being laced with carfentanyl

Equilibrium and Homeostasis

What fuels the compulsion for drug-seeking behavior once addiction has occurred? There are basically two processes involved. One of the functions of the brain is to maintain equilibrium (homeostasis). Drugs are taken to reduce tension and discomfort, regardless of the source of tension or of the discomfort. When the effect of the drug wears off, we are returned to a state of tension the brain is required to resolve. In doing so, the brain alerts the mind that action is required, in the same way water and food tension are alerted by an increase in bio-physiological tension. The mind has acquired ways to resolve the biological tension through trial and error (learning), much as we drink and eat to reduce those tension states. Tension-reduction strategies from addictive psychotropics become survival strategies that the mind is required to resolve. This is one of *those unconscious processes that launch the tension-reduction domain of the brain*. When you are experiencing withdrawal, an uncomfortable state, removing the unpleasantness of withdrawal is imperative. Withdrawal is a punishment for upsetting the balance of psychotropics. Removing a negative physical and affective state is a negative reinforcement that is positively reinforcing. This cycle becomes part of the reward system as well as the tension-reduction system involved in homeostasis. To borrow a phrase, "a mind is a terrible thing to waste."

Once Again, Why Are Illicit Drugs Consumed?

Illicit drugs are consumed because, chemically, they act like the neurotransmitters our brain produces. They occupy the same receptor sites in the brain. Addiction to OxyContin is not appreciably different than addiction to heroin, morphine, or *endorphins*, the "feel-good" psychotropic we produce naturally. Chemically, they look similar to our brain's receptors. The difference is our brains produce chemicals in moderation on an *as-needed basis*, and addicts introduce them into the system *continuously* without allowing the brain to go through the normal process of making an adjustment to the neurotransmitter that has been released. In the normal process, when the neurotransmitters are broken down and reabsorbed, the delicate balance is maintained. A chemical balance is created, and the brain returns to homeostasis. This is obviously a gross oversimplification of how neurotransmitters are produced, processed, and reabsorbed.

It is most important to understand that the chemicals we are discussing activate the receptors in the brain that alter mood. For example, serotonin is a chemical that makes us feel good when we use a drug like cocaine. Why and how? Cocaine is an SSRI (selective serotonin reuptake inhibitor). SSRIs are prescribed for people with a depressed mood. SSRIs restrict serotonin being reabsorbed into the system, producing an enhanced mood. What that means is that it's not the cocaine that makes us high; it is, instead, the serotonin flooding our brain. Cocaine does not allow the brain to maintain homeostasis by occupying the sites that would reabsorb the serotonin. When the *appropriately prescribed medical dosage* level is obtained and maintained, there is no increase in the SSRI. This is not the case with cocaine; tolerance develops an increase in the amount of cocaine required to reach the same state.

In the case of abuse, as each level of cocaine becomes *habituated*, the addict increases the amount of cocaine in a never-ending cycle. Habituation is the body's response when the amount used fails to produce the desired result. When individuals using the mood-altering substance recognize that they are not obtaining the desired outcome, *they have several options: take more of what they are taking, try a new drug, or acknowledge that they have become addicted and need to either quit or seek treatment.* Remember, addiction has occurred when you are taking the drug to avoid withdrawal. Basic credit for the list goes to Zak Fellows,[92] who created it as a class handout for a class he was teaching at MIT. I have added and updated in some areas.

What Are Some of the Most Commonly Abused Drugs, and What Are Their Mental Effects?

Unfortunately, two of the most lethal drugs are legal: alcohol and nicotine. Collectively, they account for over half a million deaths per year. The following drugs are included because they are psychoactive. The drugs will be discussed by the way they affect the brain/mind.

Sedatives

Alcohol is particularly dangerous because it affects multiple organs in the body. Alcohol can be processed by most adult human beings at approximately one ounce per hour without producing severe intoxication. Go beyond that, and when alcohol begins to accumulate in the body faster than the body systems can process it, the effect is intoxication. When individuals with depressive problems are prescribed medications, they are cautioned not to drink with those medications, because alcohol is a central nervous system depressant. Therefore, if you're already depressed and you ingest a drug that will add to that depression, it is not difficult to understand why so many suicides are committed with the assistance of alcohol.

Alcohol is a mild euphoric; it calms you, decreases your inhibitions, and is relaxing. Many social drinkers and alcoholics choose it because it makes them more comfortable in social settings or it allows them to behave in ways that their mind will not allow when sober. It removes the critical parent part of the mind reminds us not to look foolish. But after a few drinks, you are willing to wear the lampshade, sing at the karaoke bar, engage in conversation with members of the opposite sex, and feel comfortable talking to them.

Moderate drinkers, those who monitor the rate at which they consume alcohol, don't make poor decisions about drinking and driving. Usually they are not harmed. Those who choose not to recognize their increased dependence on the mental side effects of their alcohol consumption have stepped onto the slippery slope leading to alcoholism. It is unfortunate that alcohol, one of the most harmful drugs available, is not considered a drug and is cheap and readily available. Interestingly, alcoholics consider themselves to be better than drug addicts.

A major concern with excessive alcohol consumption is its effect on so many organs of the body. As such, it may very well be the most harmful drug of all. For a complete list of its effects on the body, I recommend some independent research; it would take several pages here to address all the physiological issues created by alcohol consumption. Side effects are the same as those for benzodiazepines (see below) plus nausea, vomiting, breathing suppression, terrible withdrawal (including psychosis seizures), brain damage, various diseases, and death.

Benzodiazepines
Substances include diazepam (Valium), clonazepam (Klonopin), lorazepam (Ativan), temazepam (Restoril), flunitrazepam (Rohypnol), triazolam (Halcion), and alprazolam (Xanax). "Benzos" have the effect of producing calm, relaxed muscles and making you sleepy. Side effects include drowsiness, falls, impaired coordination, impaired memory, and dizziness.

Benzodiazepine Agonists
Substances include zolpidem (Ambien), eszopiclone (Lunesta), zopiclone, zaleplon (Sonata). Agonists are drugs that react with the receptor site that produce similar effects as benzodiazepines. For most, these drugs just cause them to become sleepy, but some experience hallucinations and sleeplike states. Side effects are the same as those for benzodiazepines.

Barbiturates
Substances include phenobarbital, pentobarbital, thiopental (sodium pentothal, sodium amytal), and secobarbital. They effect a sense of calm euphoria and sleepiness. Side effects are the same as those for benzodiazepines but also include breathing suppression, terrible withdrawal, and death.

Gammahydroxybutyrates (GHB)
These substances effect euphoria, energy, or sleepiness (a mix of stimulant and sedative effects). Side effects are the same as those for benzodiazepines but also include nausea, vomiting, breathing suppression, psychosis, seizures, and death.

Stimulants
Amphetamines:

Substances include amphetamine (Adderall), methamphetamine (Desoxyn), methylphenidate (Ritalin), phentermine, 4-methyllaminorex, phenmetrazine (Preludin), meth cathinone, fenfluramine (Pondemin, Fen-Phen), dexfenfluramine (Redux), pseudoephedrine (Sudafed), ephedrine, phenylpropanolamine (old Triaminic), and phenylephrine (Sudafed PE). They produce euphoria, energy, the ability to work, enhanced concentration, appetite suppression, and the ability to stay awake. Side effects include anxiety, paranoia, psychosis, high blood pressure, heart attack, stroke, and brain damage (when used excessively). One of the unfortunate solutions to these side effects is to limit or modulate them by adding heroin or other depressants to the amphetamine.

Narcotics

Substances include MDMA (ecstasy), MDA, and MDEA. They produce euphoria; energy; deep and unusual thoughts; perceived inspiration and novelty; enhanced sex; and a heightened response to dancing, music, art, and the senses. They can boost contentment and connection to other people and strong emotions. Side effects are the same as those for amphetamines but also include brain damage, confusion, agitation, death due to hyperthermia, heart attack, water intoxication, and other problems.

Cocaine

Effects are the same as those for amphetamines. Side effects are the same as those for amphetamines but also include an increased risk of heart attack.

Full Opioid Agonists

Substances include morphine, heroin (diacetylmorphine), hydrocodone (Vicodin), oxycodone (Percocet, OxyContin), Fentanyl, Demerol, codeine, opium, hydromorphone (Dilaudid), oxymorphone (Opana), and methadone. They are used as pain relievers, calming agents, relaxants, sleep inducers, and appetite suppressors. Side effects include nausea, constipation, vomiting, drowsiness, and breathing suppression. Carfentanil is a recent addition to the opiate use group. It is a large animal tranquilizer (elephants and rhinoceros) and 50-100 more times more potent than fentanyl. It is being used to enhance the effects of heroin and killing indiscriminately because of its' potency.

Partial, Selective, or Mixed Opioid Agonists

Substances include buprenorphine (Suboxone, which contains naloxone, an opioid antagonist), pentazocine, nalbuphine, tramadol (Ultram), and tifluadon. Subutex is only buprenorphine. They effect pain relief and a sensation that is not quite as euphoric or relaxing as the full agonists above. Side effects include nausea, constipation, vomiting, and drowsiness.

Cannabis

This substance is primarily tetrahydrocannabinol and some other active ingredients, like cannabidiol in smaller quantities. It effects unusual thoughts and feelings and sometimes induces calmness, happiness, hunger, and an enhanced appreciation of art. Side effects include impairment of memory, thinking, reflexes, and coordination. Cannabis may contribute to psychosis in the long term. It may also relieve nausea, vomiting, and neuropathic pain.

There is much controversy now as to whether marijuana should be a Schedule-1 narcotic. Does it deserve the same treatment as heroin and cocaine? I am unfamiliar with any literature that indisputably supports the premise that it contributes to psychosis. Despite the fact that several states have decriminalized marijuana, cannabis is still a federal crime as a Schedule-1 narcotic. It does have serious implications for young developing minds and may account for some gray-matter loss in adolescents and contribute to frontal-lobe (decision-making) issues.

Psychedelics
Phenethylamines

Substances include mescaline (peyote cactus), 2 C-Series drugs, and DO series drugs. They effect a feeling of novelty, inspiration, or reverence; fast, disordered thoughts or trances; perceptual anomalies (patterns can move, colors become brighter, "seeing" sounds, "smelling" colors); and crazy ideas and beliefs. Side effects include anxiety, insomnia, paranoia, and temporary psychosis. They may contribute to psychosis in the long term or cause flashbacks (HP PD). Some also cause nausea, increased body temperature, and tremors.

Tryptamines

Substances include psilocybin and psilocin (found in mushrooms), bufotenin (in toads), DMT (in plants), 5-MeO-DMT (in plants), 5-MeO-Ti PT, DET, AMT, and 4-HO-DiPT. Effects are the same as those for mescaline. Side effects are also the same as those for mescaline.

Ergolines

Substances include lysergic acid diethylamine (LSD) and LSA (or Dean, in plants). Effects are the same as above but can be exaggerated depending on frequency of use and dose. Side effects are the same as above too.

Dissociative Anesthetics

Substances include phencyclidine (PCP), dextromethorphan, and ketamine. They effect a feeling of distance from reality and body, numbing of sensations in pain, and convincing and absorbing hallucinations Side effects include nausea, vomiting, coma, violence, extreme confusion, and temporary psychosis. PCP causes brain damage.

Deliriants

Substances include scopolamine and atropine (in plants), diphenhydramine (Benadryl), and dimenhydrinate (Dramamine). They produce a loss of memory and convincing and absorbing hallucinations. Side effects include extreme confusion; temporary psychosis; hot, dry skin; dry mouth; huge pupillary dilation; fast heartbeat; and death.

Inhalants (Huffing)

Substances include diethyl ether (starter fluid), toluene, gasoline, glue, paint, xenon, Freon, halothane, and sevoflurane. They effect relaxation, euphoria, pain relief, hallucinations, and strange sensations. Different inhalants cause different effects. Side effects include many diseases, death, nausea, vomiting, accidental asphyxiation, and falls, though they vary depending on the particular drug.

Nitrous Oxide

Substances effect calm, euphoria, pain relief, memory loss, and unconsciousness. Side effects are similar to those above.

Nitrites

Substances include isoamyl nitrite and isobutyl nitrite. They produce a head rush, muscle relaxation, and dizziness. Side effects include dangerously low blood pressure and fainting.

Other Drugs Not Fitting the Above Classification Scheme

It would not have been particularly convincing for me to simply say the drugs of abuse produce effects that are positive for those who abuse them. If you examine the effects of the primary drugs of abuse, it will be obvious that they make the world "go away" in multiple and different ways. From a learning point of view, we know what's reinforcing based on what an organism is willing to work for. The end result of the utilization of the drugs listed above is a combination of effects including dissociation from self, excitement, enhanced self-esteem, personality alteration, and altering of emotions. It is important to remember that those who have reached the state of addiction found it more acceptable to be in their altered state than in the state they were in before they began altering their minds.

Nicotine

The cigarette companies call cigarettes "a delivery system for nicotine." To enhance the effects, they have added accelerants like ammonia to help the nicotine cross the blood-brain barrier more quickly. Again for emphasis, the oft ignored and little-known fact is, that milligram per milligram, *nicotine is more addictive than heroin*. Most addicts, when they come into treatment, are willing to give up their illicit drug or their licit drug (alcohol), but they are not willing to give up nicotine. Nicotine is a stimulant and a mild euphoric. Unfortunately, the effects of nicotine are similar in duration to the effects of crack cocaine; the effects last only for approximately twenty to sixty minutes, barely twice that of crack cocaine. Most smokers consume approximately one pack of cigarettes a day. When you assume eight hours of sleep, two hours for eating, and another hour for incidentals, that leaves thirteen hours to smoke twenty cigarettes—or one cigarette every thirty-nine minutes! Agitation begins to set in, in anticipation of that smoke break, and escalates because the brain and mind are expecting their dose. Women consuming nicotine should beware—*nicotine accounts for the majority of deaths among women*.

Electronic cigarettes (e-cigs) are the newest innovation in the nicotine delivery system. They have not been around long enough for us to know what the long-term effects of this particular delivery system will be on humans. There have already been reports of battery explosions and metals in the oil. They are billed as an improvement, due to the removal of some of the contaminants in tobacco cigarettes that are potential carcinogens. I have not compared the amount of nicotine available in a single drag of an e-cig to that of tobacco. Could it provide more nicotine than traditional cigarettes, thereby increasing habituation and requiring increased amounts of the psychoactive substance? The fact that they are flavored makes them more palatable to youth.

Marijuana is usually touted and maligned as *the gateway drug*. In reality, nicotine and alcohol are the far more dangerous drugs here, as both are legal and therefore easily accessible. Most drug use begins with these two legal mind-altering substances.

Spice, K2, Black Mamba, and Others
Substances include methaqualone (Quaaludes, Sopor), thalidomide, meprobromate (Miltown), carisoprodol (Soma), glutethimide, chloral hydrate (knockout drops, Mickey), ethchlorvynol (Placidyl), methyprylon, and primidone.

Spice and bath salts are new and dangerous entries onto the illicit substance list. The active ingredient is a synthetic cannabinoid that is manufactured in China and the United States; it is sprayed on vegetable material and packaged under the names above. The unfortunate thing is that the chemical composition is not known. Each time the chemicals that are psychotropic are identified and added to the list of illegal drugs, the manufacturers change the formula slightly. Florida, in particular, has attempted to identify and predict the products that will be used to produce the high, but they cannot get ahead of the manufacturers. Spice does produce a high similar to marijuana, but its chemical composition is far more dangerous. The medical community does not know how to treat medical complications because they don't know what chemicals might be causing symptoms; the ingredients vary almost by batch of the product. This product is far more dangerous than marijuana and is producing increasing admissions to the hospital psychiatric units and even deaths.

Summary of Psychotropics
This fairly inclusive but not exhaustive listing of the major psychotropics of abuse is to alert the portion of the community to drugs of abuse that may be available in the family medicine cabinet. In particular, adolescents are prone to taking these pharmaceuticals. Members of the family who have a predilection to prescription drug abuse are more than happy to help themselves to anything available in the medicine cabinets of their family and friends. In the review of the drugs of abuse that are legal, I intend to make it known that they mimic those drugs that are illegal. Your awareness may keep psychotropics from being available to those who may wish to experiment or those

who are already addicted. In the absence of availability of an addict's preferred drug(s) of abuse, any mind-altering substance will do to avoid withdrawal.

The notion that drugs of abuse "hijack the brain" does not hold up in the face of the decision made by hardcore addicts and alcoholics to voluntarily cease the use of their drug(s) of abuse. They are willing to endure the discomfort of detoxification. Currently, there are drugs available that ease the physical discomfort. When they make the decision to seek help, they provide cognitive reasons for their choice to abstain. Fear of death or disease, recognition that they have given up their former lives, fear of disappointing family, loss of occupation, legal complications, poverty, medical complications of long-term use, and frequent incarceration are all signposts to the destination AA and NA attribute to "reaching their bottom." If they relapse following that, the explanation is that they didn't really "reach their bottom." It is my contention that the treating community failed to fix what was actually broken: their *thinking disorder*.

CHAPTER 10

Summaries

To Addicts and Those Who Care

For those of you who are in recovery, those contemplating recovery, and especially those of you who are still in the throes of addiction, this book may make you better consumers of addiction-treatment products. In the addiction community, there are products to choose from called best practices—those products that have proven to be more likely to produce the result you seek. When you have tried a product and it has not produced the desired result, it may be that you are not willing to give up your psychic pain reliever because you don't know that psychic pain is *why* you use. I don't find it useful to castigate you for not being at your "final bottom." I find it more useful to aid you in your search of the rationale that gives you permission and directs you to hurt yourself. It is amazing that you go to the lengths you do to obtain help. The therapeutic community needs to recognize that you are solving the problem in the only way you know how. Aftercare is critical, especially for those of you who opted out of the non-addicted community.

Reentering the general culture when you have been out for a long time is difficult. The theme song to *Cheers*—an '80s sitcom set in a bar—says it best:

Sometimes you wanna go
Where everybody knows your name,
And they're always glad you came.
You wanna be where you can see our troubles are all the same;
You wanna go where everybody knows your name.

It's far easier to commiserate with those who know what the life of addiction recovery is all about. Unfortunately, many of those who would welcome you back want you to deal with your troubles in the same way you used to

Summary for Treatment Professionals, Lay Treatment Staff, and Sponsors

These three basic facts are what led me to question the status quo:

- The number of deaths related to substance abuse (25 percent of deaths annually in the United States are attributed to nicotine and alcohol). Should I conclude that there are seventy-five million addicts in the United States, and that explains why they account for 25 percent of the annual death rate?
- What accounts for the number of "biologically diseased addicts" who voluntarily gave up addictive substances to come into treatment? Must I conclude that either they were a subpopulation of addicts who did not have the disease but abused drugs anyway or that they were not representative of the abusing subculture? When I took at their histories, the vast majority were suffering from a variety of early maladaptive schemas, abuse and neglect in their many forms, poor or maladaptive child rearing, and numerous ACEs. Do not construe this as a blanket indictment of parents; it is not. Many were victims of abuse from other external sources, including but not limited to rejection from their peers at school. Many misconstrued their treatment, because young children do not have the cognitive skills to accurately interpret events that occur around them. You don't have to be the victim to have PTSD; *it's enough to observe someone being victimized.*
- Our success rate with the current disease model is extremely low. We blame the addict for not having reached his or her bottom, for not following the formula, for not having worked the steps properly, or for failing to resolve character defects. Is it possible that we are dealing with a software (mind) rather than a hardware (brain) issue? Many of the patients who present for treatment have members of their family who gave up their addiction voluntarily and without help. They wonder why they have not been able to do the same. They assume that since they are genetically related they should have the same ability. Only when they realize that despite the fact they grew up in the same household they did not live in the same phenomenal world. Would

AA/NA say that, if they did it without following the formula, were they really addicts or did they actually have the disease? Is the disease defined by only being responsive to AA for treatment?

This may be particularly offensive to those of you who are committed to the *disease model*. Regardless of where you acquired your addiction schema (school, graduate school, through AA or NA, or through your own recovery), you *know* how *you* obtained and maintain *your* recovery. In the absence of a competing model, I understand why you would object to the thinking disorder premise. It worked for you and confirms your schema about addiction. To those who are recovering or recovered, I would ask you to recall the initial step you took. Did you or did you not have to make the *conscious decision* to stop taking your drug(s) of choice to participate in a recovery program? If so, how can you hold on to the premise that it is a *biological disease*, not a *thinking disease*? I understand that this is a direct assault on perhaps the core of your schema regarding addiction. I understand that, as treating professionals, it is comforting to hold on to the belief that the non-responsive addict simply hadn't reached their bottom, and it isn't your lack of knowledge or skill that failed to dissuade them from relapse. After all, the most prestigious institutions of our government (NIDA and NIAAA) define addiction as a *chronically relapsing brain disease*.

What is not understood is that the disease model came into being at a time when we had no alternative model to compete with it. In the absence of a competing model, the only explanation that made sense was AA, which had a twenty- or thirty-year head start over the bio/psychological/social model in working with the disorder. The disease model went from *hypothesis* to *fact* without empirical testing. The intransigence of the behaviors associated with addiction supported the notion that it must be the correct model. Those physicians who successfully treated addiction medically were forced to abandon that treatment by the government, in favor of the mentally hijacking "reefer madness" theory, which was part and parcel of the war on drugs.

Once we think we have the answer, we stop looking. Since the Copernican Revolution, most of us have accepted that the Earth rotates around the sun. I understand that when you just want to do your job and apply what you think you know, there is little time to ask, "Is this actually working?" Substance abusers are treatable—if you have the right manual for the treatment of substance abusers. What is your schema for addiction? Is it producing reliable results?

Funding Agencies

The allocation of resources is critical to our ability to successfully understand and treat substance abuse.

To have a meaningful dialogue on the amelioration of the substance-abuse issue, we must reduce our reliance (at least for the moment) on the schema that addiction is a biological disease. Our current asset allocations are primarily directed at interdiction and substantiation of the disease model. How do we expect to stop the influx of illicit drugs across our borders when we haven't discovered what makes illicit drugs the preferred choice? With our war on drugs, we have created organizations that recognize the wealth creation of supplying illicit substances, and they will continue providing supply as long as demand exists. Our substitution of licit drugs (e.g., methadone, Suboxone, and buprenorphine) for illicit narcotics is not a cure.

The belief that substance-abuse treatment will be successful when we find the right chemical cocktail will simply spur on Big Pharma to gobble up valuable resources and limit the exploration of how we might successfully treat this thinking disease. I am not suggesting that continuing to explore antagonists for narcotics and psychoactive substances be abandoned. There are treatment protocols that facilitate detox, that serve to assist in avoiding cravings and block opiate-receptor sites (e.g., Narcan and Naloxone), that aid in the treatment of addiction. Besides CBT, what about EMDR, psychodrama, meditation, mindfulness, and other mind-body strategies that repair dysregulation?

We know from the brain-imaging studies that brains return to normal over time, but it is not a few weeks or months. Sometimes it takes years. We know that reinforcing competing behaviors (e.g., theater tickets) for clean UAs reduces relapse and re-wires the brain, thereby reinforcing new circuitry. We know that aftercare is critical to recovery, yet there are no long-term studies of what aftercare should look like. There are no RFPs for the assessment of the effects of various treatment aftercare regimens. Why? There are no comparisons of therapeutic communities, their core programs and the relationship of those programs to treatment success.[93]

I am asking funding-agency decision makers who have never questioned their addiction schema to look at the observations of addicts who dispute the disease model with their behavior. The loss to families and the country, economically and emotionally, as well as the disproportionate contribution of this population through death and disease, would suggest a rigorous scientific evaluation of new treatment strategies and a new direction for establishing both cause and treatment efficacy. Please ask yourself if your schema needs updating.

The costs to the budget, loss of productivity, destruction of families, and repetition of familial addiction all create a need to review our prevailing schema regarding addiction. We must test the hypothesis that this a thinking disease, not a biological disease.

NOTES

1. Sally Satel and Scott O. Lilienfeld, "Addiction and the Brain-Disease Fallacy," Frontiers in Psychiatry, Volume 4 Number 141 2013. Published Online 2014, March 3. doi:10: 3389/fpst.2013.00140 in Sally Satel and Scott O. Lilienfeld, *Brainwashed: The Seductive Appeal of Mindless Neuroscience* Reprinted by permission of Basic Books, a member of The Perseus Books Group. 2014

2. Centers for Disease Control and Prevention, "Smoking and Tobacco Use: Fast Facts," Cigarette smoking is responsible for more than 480,000/year. Page last reviewed December 20, 2016   https://www.cdc.gov/tobacco/data_statistics/fact_sheets/fast_facts/.

3. Centers for Disease Control and Prevention, "Alcohol Deaths," last revised https://www.cdc.gov/features/alcohol-deaths/index.html.

4. National Institute on Drug Abuse (NIDA), "Overdose Death Rates," NIH, last revised 2015, https://www.drugabuse.gov/.../trends-statistics/overdose-death-rates.

5. National Institute on Drug Abuse (NIDA), "The Science of Drug Abuse and Addiction: The Basics," NIDA (2016) Media Guide. Retrieved April 1, 2017, from https://www.drugabuse.gov/publications/media-guide.

6. 6. NIH Drug Facts Genetics and Epigenetics of Addiction. Retrieved April 1, 2017/ from https://www.drugabuse.gov/publications/drugfacts/genetics-epigenetics-addiction

7. N. M. Hesselbrock et al., "Genetics and Alcoholism: The COGA Project."] (2001): in D. P. Agurual and H. K. Seitz, eds., "Alcohol in Health and Disease," 103-124 New York: Marcel Dekker,

8. American Society of Addictive Medicine (ASAM), "Definition of Addiction, Adopted by the Board of Directors April 19th, 2011http://www.asam.org/quality-practice/definition-of-addiction.

9. V. J. Felitti et al., "Relationship of Childhood Abuse and Household Dysfunction to Many Leading Causes of Death in Adults," *American Journal of Preventative Medicine* 14, no. 4 (1998): 245-258.

10. S. D. Spragg, "Morphine Addiction in Chimpanzees," *Comparative Psychological Monographs* 15 (1940): 1–132.

11. M. A. Nader and W. L. Wolverton, "Effects of Increasing the Magnitude of an Alternative Reinforcer on Drug Choice in a Discrete Trial's Choice Procedure," *Psychopharmacology* 5, no. 2 (1991): 169–74, http://link.springer.com/article/10.1007% 2FBF02244304.

12. "Naltrexone," Wikipedia, last revised January 3, 2017, https://en.wikipedia.org/wiki/Naltrexone this page last modified on 3 January 2017, at 19:26

13. Anne M. Fletcher, *Inside Rehab*, (New York: Viking Press, 2013).

14. M. Ferri, L. Amato, and M. Davoli, "Alcohol Anonymous and Other 12-Step Programs for Alcohol Dependence," *Cochrane Database of Systematic Reviews* 3 (July 19, 2006); L. A. Kaskutas, "Alcoholics Anonymous Effectiveness: Faith Meets Science," *Journal of . Addictive Diseases*. 28, no. 2 (2009): 145–57.; L.A. Kaskutas, "Alcoholics Anonymous Effectiveness: Faith Meets Science, Journal of Addictive Diseases, Volume 28, no 2 (2009): 145-157; J. M. Brandsma, M. C. Maultsby Jr., and R. J. Welsh, *Outpatient Treatment of Alcoholism: A Review and Comparative Study*, (Baltimore: University Park Press, 1980).

15. "Dr. Vivek Murthy, Surgeon General," *The Dr. Oz Show*, aired November 10, 2015 (CBS).

16. Vivek Murthy, "Chronic Disease Model," (lecture, Association of Health Care Journalists Center for Excellence, Cleveland, OH, April 9, 2016).

17. Frances E. Jensen, *The Teenage Brain*, (New York: Harper Collins, 2015), 37–38.

18. Jeffery Young, *Cognitive Therapy for Personality Disorders: A Schema Focused Approach*, 3rd ed., (Sarasota, FL: Professional Resource Press, 1999).

19. American Psychiatric Association, *Diagnostic and Statistical Manual of Mental Disorders*, 5th ed., (Arlington, VA: American Psychiatric Association, 2013).

20. APA (American Psychiatric Association)' Medscape, Wednesday, March 29, 2017; Alcoholism Is Not What It Used to Be. Medscape www.medscape.com

21. P. Cohen and J. Cohen J, "The Clinician's Illusion," *Archives of General Psychiatry* 12 (1984): 1178-1182, doi: 1001/archpsyc.1984.01790230064010.

22. D. A. Ciraulo, J. Piechniczek-Buczek, and E. N. Iscan, "Outcome Predictors in Substance Use Disorders," *Psychiatric Clinicians of North America.* 26, no. 2 (2013): 381–409.

23. Joshua P. Smith and Sarah W. Book, "Comorbidity of Generalized Anxiety Disorder and Alcohol Use Disorders among Individuals Seeking Outpatient Substance Abuse Treatment," *Addictive Behavior* 35, no. 1 (2003): 42–5, doi: 10.1016/j. addbeh.2009.07.002.

24. S. B. Quello, Kathleen T. Brady, and Susan C. Sonne, "Mood Disorders and Substance Use Disorder: A Complex Comorbidity," *Scientific Practice Perspective* 3, no. 1 (2005): 13–21, http://www.ncbi.nlm.nih.gov/pmc/articles/PMC2851027.

25. S. H. Stewart and P. J. Conrod, eds. *Anxiety and Substance Use Disorders: The Vicious Cycle of Comorbidity,* (New York: Springer, 2008).

26. D. A. Regier et al. "Comorbidity of Mental Disorders with Alcohol and Other Drug Abuse," *Journal of the American Medical Association* 264, no. 19 (1990): 2511–18.

27. R. C. Kessler et al., "Lifetime and 12-month Prevalence of DSM-III-R Psychiatric Disorders in the United States: Results from the National Comorbidity Survey." *Archives of General Psychiatry* 51 (1994): 8–19.

28. R. C. Kessler et al., "Lifetime Prevalence and Age-of-Onset Distribution of DSM-IV Disorders in the National Comorbidity Survey Replication," *Archives of General. Psychiatry* 62, no. 6 (2005): 593–602.

29. M.G. Kushner et al., "Epidemiological Perspectives on Co-occurring Anxiety Disorder and Substance Use Disorder," in S. H. Stewart and P. J. Conrod, eds., *Anxiety and Substance Use Disorders: The Vicious Cycle of Comorbidity,* (New York: Springer, 2008), 3-17.

30. M. G. Kushner, K. J. Sher, and B. D. Beitman, "The Relation between Alcohol Problems and the Anxiety Disorders," *American Journal of Psychiatry* 147, vol. 6 (1990): 685–95.

31. *Comorbidity: Addiction and Other Mental Ilnesses* NIDA; National Institute of Health. U.S. Department of Health and Human Services. This Page last updated March 2011. NIH Publication Number 10-5771, Printed December 2008, Revised September 2010 www.drugabuse.gov>publications/ResearchReports

32. Maia Szalavitz, *Unbroken Brain: A Revolutionary New Way of Understanding Addiction,* (2016). ST. MARTIN'S PRESS NEW YORK

33. Centers for Disease Control (CDC), Injury Prevention & Control: Division of Violence Prevention. ACE Study by Kaiser Permanente Health Appraisal Clinic in San Diego, California, and the Centers for Disease Control and Prevention from 1995-1997 http://www.cdc.gov/ace/index.htm. Page last reviewed April 1, 2016

34. Substance Abuse and Mental Health Services Administration, *Results from the National Survey on Drug Use and Health Findings*, NSDUH Series H-42, HHS Publication No. (SMA) 11-4667. Rockville, MD 2012

35. Community Recovery Program, The Salvation Army's City of Hope in Sarasota, Florida. www.salvationarmyflorida.org/sarasota

36. NIH News, National Institute of Health, National Institute of Alcohol Abuse & Addiction (NIAAA). *NIAAA Reports Project MATCH Main Findings,* NEWS RELEASE, FOR IMMEDIATE RELEASE, Tuesday December 17, 1996. http://www.niaaa.nih.gov.

37. Johann Hari, *Chasing the Scream: The First and Last Days of the War on Drugs,* (New York: Bloomsbury, 2015).

38. 38. B. K. Alexander et al., "Effect of Early and Later Colony Housing on Oral Ingestion of Morphine in Rats," (1981) *Pharmacology Biochemistry and Behavior* 15, no. 4:571-576.

39. L. Robins et al., "Narcotic Use in Southeast Asia and Afterward," *Archives of General Psychiatry* 32 (1975): 955–6.

40. Virginia E. Davis and Michael J. Walsh, "Alcohol, Amines, and Alkaloids: A Possible Biochemical Basis for Alcohol Addiction," *Science* New Series Volume 167 **No.**

3920 (Feb. 13, 1970), pp1005-1007 Published by American Association for the Advancement of Science 1005–7, 1doi: 10.1126/science.167.3920.1005.

41. The HAMS Network, "Myths from Drug and Alcohol Rehab," http://www.hamsnetwork.org/myths/.

42. L. Bevilacqua and D. Goldman, "Genes and Addiction," *Clinical Pharmacological Therapy* 85, no. 4 (2009): 359–61.

43. K. S. Kendler et al., "Genetic and Environmental Influences on Alcohol, Caffeine, Cannabis, and Nicotine Use from Early Adolescence to Middle Adulthood," *Archives of General Psychiatry* 65 (2008): 674–82.

44. Bruce K. Alexander, "The Rise and Fall of the Official View of Addiction," last revised July 3, 2014, http://www.brucekalexander.com[45].

45. Jeffery Young, *Cognitive Therapy for Personality Disorders*: A schema Focused Approach (third edition) Sarasota Florida: Professional Resource Press, 1999

46. S. H. Ahmed et al., "Neurobiology of Addiction versus Drug Use Driven by Lack of Choice," *Current Opinion in. Neurobiology.* 295, no. 17 (2013); 2003–0017, http://dx.doi.org/10.1016/j.conb.2013.01.02806.

47. Lance Dodes, MD and Zachary Dodes *The Sober Truth: Debunking the Bad Science Behind Twelve-Step Programs and the Rehab Industry*, (Boston, MA: Beacon Press, 2014).

48. Gabrielle Glaser, *The False Gospel of Alcoholics Anonymous*, (Atlantic, 2015), 50-60. The Atlantic Monthly Group, 600 New Hampshire Ave, NW, Washington DC 20037

49. L. Robins et al., "Narcotic Use in Southeast Asia and Afterwards," *Archives of General Psychiatry* 32 (1975): 955–61.

50. Bessel van der Kolk, *The Body Keeps Score*, (New York: Viking Press, 2015).

51. *Alcoholics Anonymous*, 4th ed., Alcoholics Anonymous World Services Inc. New York City, 2001. http://www.aa.org

52. K. E. Watkins et al., "An Effectiveness Trial of Group Cognitive Behavioral Therapy for Patients with Persistent Depressive Symptoms in Substance Abuse Treatment," *Archives of General Psychiatry* 68, no. 6 (2011): 577–84. 53.

54. D. C. Walsh et al., "A Randomized Trial of Treatment Options for Alcohol Abusing Workers," *New England Journal of Medicine* 325, no. 11 (1991): 775–82.

55. L. A. Kaskutas, "alcoholics Annonymous Effectiveness: Faith Meets Science," Journal of Addictive Diseases, Volume 28, no 2 (2009) 145-147

56. A. I. Leshner, "Addiction Is a Brain Disease, and It Matters," *Science* 278 (1997): 45–47. http:/www.ncbi.nlm.nih.gov/pubmed/9311924.

57. G. M. Heyman, "On the Science of Substance Abuse," *Science* 208, no. 5365 (May 8, 1998): 803, doi: 10.1126/science.280.5363.803e.

58. G. M. Heyman, "Addiction and Choice: Theory and New Data," *Frontiers in Psychiatry* (May 6, 2013), http://journal.frontiersin.org/article/10.3389/fpsyt.2013.00031/full.

59. Franklin Ernst Jr., 1964, http://ernstokcorral.com/OK_Corral.html.

60. Frederick C. Bartlett, *Remembering: A Study in Experimental and Social Psychology*, (Cambridge: Cambridge University Press, 1932).

61. Jean Piaget, "Piaget's Theory of Cognitive Development," Wikipedia, Last updated April 1, 2017 https://en.wikipedia.org/wiki/Piaget's_theory_of_cognitive_development. last accessed April 2, 2017

62. George Kelly, *The Psychology of Personal Constructs*, (New York: Norton, 1955).

63. B.F. Skinner, *Science and Human Behavior*, (New York: MacMillan, 1958). Visit: http://en.wikipedia.org/wiki/B._F._Skinner.

64. Aaron T. Beck, *Cognitive Therapy and the Emotional Disorders*, (Madison, CT: International Universities Press, Inc., 1975). Visit: http://en.wikipedia.org/wiki/Cognitive_therapy.

65. Katherine Nelson, *Language in Cognitive Development Emergence of the Mediated Mind*, (Cambridge: Cambridge University Press, 1996).

66. John Locke, *An Essay Concerning Human Understanding* 1689, https://en.wikipedia.org/wiki/John_Locke.

67. Schema(psychology)-Wikipedia https://en.wikipedia.org/wiki/Schema_(psychology).

68. Adverse Childhood Experience (ACE) Study, Longitudinal Studies of Child Abuse and Neglect LONGSCAN and the National Survey of Child and Adolescent Well-Being NCSAW. ACF/OPRE 2012 B. Child Welfare Information Gateway. https://www.childwelfare.gov/pubspdf/long_term_consequences.pdf

69. V. J. Felliti and R. Anda, "The Relationship of Adverse Childhood Experiences to Adult Medical Disease, Psychiatric Disorders, and Sexual Behavior: Implications for Health Care," in R. Lanius, E. Vermetton, and C. Pain, eds., *The Hidden Epidemic: The Impact of Early Life Trauma on Health and Disease*, Chapter 8, pp77-87, (2010) Cambridge University Press The Edinburgh Building, Cambridge CB2 8RU, UK.

70. T. Messmen-Morre, K. Walsh, and D. Dellilo, "*Emotion Dysregulation and Risky Sexual Behavior in Revictimizatio*n," *Child Abuse and Neglect* 34, no. 12 (2016): 967–76.

72. B. Perry, "Supporting Maltreated Children: Countering the Effects of Neglect and Abuse," *Adoption Advocate* (2012), ADOPTION_ADVOCATE_NO 48. pdf. pp1-5 This article was first published in the North American Council on Adoptable Children's (NACAC) Summer 2011 issue of "Adoptalk" and is reprinted with permission. It has been adapted from articles by Bruce Perry, MD, PhD, senior fellow at the Child Trauma Academy (www.childtrauma.org).

73. J. Gold, M. Wolan Sullivan, and M. Lewis, "The Relationship between Abuse and Violent Delinquency: The Conversion of Shame to Blame in Juvenile Offenders," *Child Abuse and Neglect* 35, no. 7 (2011): 459–67.

74. V.J. Felitti, "The Relation Between Adverse Childhood Experiences and Adult Health: *Turning Gold into Lead*," *The Permanente Journal* 6, no. 1 (2002).

75. Frances S. Jensen. *The Teenage Brain New York:* Harper Collins, 2015

76. J. B. Watson and R. Raynor, "Conditioned Emotional Reactions," *Journal of Experimental Psychology* 3, no. 1 (1920): 1.

77. Joseph R. Troisi II, "Perhaps More Consideration of Pavlovian-Operant Interaction May Improve the Clinical Efficacy of Behavioral-Based Drug Treatment Programs," *Psychological Record* 63, no. 4 (2013): 863–94.

78. Albert Bandura, *Social Learning Theory*, (Englewood Cliffs, NJ: Prentice Hall, 1977). Visit: http://www.verywell.com/social-learning-theory-2795074.

79. Eric Berne, *Games People Play: The Psychology of Human Relations*, (New York: GrovePress,1964).Visit:https://en.wikipedia.org/wiki/Eric_Berne_Games_People_ Play(book)

80. Abraham Maslow, "A Theory of Human Motivation," *Psychological Review* 50, no. 4 (1943): 370–96.

81. Rotter, J. B. (1966) "Generalized expectancies for internal versus external locus of control of reinforcements". *Psychological Monographs: General & applied.* 80 (1):1-28

82. "Affluenza" slammed as defense for wealthy Texas teens fatal DWI wreck. Associated Press December 12, 2013 4.32 pm Ashleigh Walsh/CBS News/ December 30, 2015, 3.47 pm. What Psychologists think of "Affluenza" defense. © 2015 CBS Interactive Inc. All Rights Reserved.

83. Dr. David Sutton, The Principle Approach 2011 Peppertree Press, LLC. 1269 First Street, Suite 7 Sarasota Florida 34236

84. John Rowan, *Subpersonalities—The People Inside Us*, (New York: Routledge, Chapman, and Hall, Inc., 1990).

85. Lawrence Kohlberg, *The Psychology of Moral Development*, (New York: Harper and Row, 1984). Visit: https://en.wikipedia.org/wiki/Lawrence_Kohlberg.

86. J. Dore, "Monologue as reenvoicement of Dialogue," in Narratives from the Crib, ed. K. Nelsen Cambridge, MS. Harvard University Press, 1989, 231-262

87. M. M. Bakhtin, *The Dialogic Imagination: Four Essays by M. M. Bakhtin*, trans. C. Emerson and M. Hoquist, (Austin: University of Texas Press, 1981). 88. Claude Steiner, *Scripts People Live*, (New York: Bantam, 1974).

89. Marina Hadži-Pešić et al., "Personality of Alcohol Addict According to the Theory of Transactional Analysis," *Procedia—Social and Behavioral Sciences* 127 (2014): 230–34.

90. Claude Steiner, *Games Alcoholics Play: The Analysis of Life Scripts*, (New York: Grove Press Inc., 1971).

91. John Baker, "Celebrate Recovery," http://www.celebraterecovery.com/index.php/about-us/about-john-baker.

92. Zakfallows. MIT, Medlinks last updated on 2012-06-08. http://zakfallows.com/static/drugchart/drugchart.html. (This is a chart that is being revised as there are new drugs to be added).

93. The Clean Slate Addiction Sight. www.cleanslate.org

94. Wayne Hall, et. al., The brain disease model of addiction: is it supported by the evidence and has it delivered on its promises? Lancet Psychiatry 2015 Volume 2: 105-10. www.thelancet.com/psychiatry Vol 2 January 2015

WHAT'S MY ACE SCORE?

<u>*Prior to Your 18th birthday*</u>

1. Did a parent or other adult in the household Often or very often... Swear at you, insult you, put you down, or humiliate you? or   Act in a way that made you afraid you might be physically be hurt? Yes or No. If Yes enter 1 _____

2. Did a parent or other adult in the household often or very often push, grab, slap or throw something at you or ever hit you so hard that you had marks or were injured?

    Yes or No If Yes enter 1_____

3. Did an adult or person at least 5 years older than you ever... Touch or fondle you or have you touch their body in a sexual way? or Attempt or actually have oral, anal, or vaginal intercourse with you? Yes or No If Yes enter 1 _____

4. Did you often or very often feel that.... No one in your family loved you or thought you were important or special? or Your family didn't look out for each other, feel close to each other, or support each other? Yes or No If Yes enter 1 _____

5. Did you often or very often feel that... You didn't have enough to eat, had to wear dirty clothes, and had no one to protect you? or Your parents were too drunk or high to take care of you or take you to the doctor if you needed it?

    Yes or No If Yes enter 1 _____

6. Was a biological parent ever lost to you through divorce, abandonment, or other reason? Yes or No If Yes enter 11 _____

7. Was your mother or stepmother : Often or very often pushed, grabbed, slapped, or had something thrown at her? or Sometimes, often or very often, kicked, bitten, hit with a fist, or hit with something hard? or Ever repeatedly hit over at least a few minutes or threatened with a gun or knife? Yes or No If Yes enter 1 _____

8. Did you live with anyone who was a problem drinker or alcoholic or who used street drugs? Yes or No If Yes enter 1 _____

9. Was a household member depressed or mentally ill or did a household member ever attempt suicide? Yes or No If Yes enter 1 _____

10. Did a household member ever go to prison? Yes or No If Yes enter 1 _____

    Add up your Yes answers and that is your ACE Score_____

Author Biography

D r. Kenneth G. Wilson is uniquely qualified to address addiction. His first contact with mental-health issues was while he was training as a military clinical-psychology specialist from 1958 to 1961—an experience that confirmed his interest in studying human behavior. He received his PhD in personality and social psychology in 1972. His next step was a role as a tenured graduate faculty assistant professor at the Center for the Study of Crime, Delinquency, and Corrections at Southern Illinois University in Carbondale, Illinois. He completed a clinical internship at the Asklepion Therapeutic Community at the US penitentiary in Marion, Illinois. This experience piqued his interest in working with hard-to-treat populations. He obtained tenured graduate faculty status, was licensed to practice psychology by examination, and was accorded drug-treatment-professional status. He left that position in 1978 to become the first police psychologist for the Denver Police Department in Colorado, which is where he obtained licensed psychologist status by examination.

To better understand the physiological response to stress that results from interactions with law enforcement, Dr. Wilson completed advanced training in biofeedback. After building it into a two-psychologist department, he left the Denver Police Department in 1982 to study the physiological and psychological effects of the isolation tank at Float to Relax, Inc. The relaxation tank wasn't widely accepted because of concerns about claustrophobia. When the company closed in 1985, Dr. Wilson went into private practice.

In 1990, he discovered the Cenikor Foundation's therapeutic community for the treatment of substance abusers. He worked part time as the clinical director and acquired his Certified Addiction Counselor III (CAC III) status. He stayed there until 1999, when he was asked to develop a clinical program to help the Stout Street Foundation

Inc. (SSF) meet state standards for a therapeutic community. SSF received its license in 1999. Dr. Wilson was then asked to take the position of clinical supervisor, and he relished the opportunity to create and supervise a truly clinically oriented program. Two years later, he became the assistant executive director/clinical director.

His tenure as a clinical supervisor provided him the opportunity to personally treat and otherwise direct the treatment of thousands of substance abusers. The position required the training and supervision of numerous addiction counselors, many of whom were professionally quite successful in their own right. Dr. Wilson retired from SSF in 2004; today, he serves as a clinical consultant and board member. His experiences as a volunteer at the Salvation Army's City of Hope CRP for substance abusers is what prompted him to write this book.